CW00525797

50 FINDS FROM BERKSHIRE

Objects from the Portable Antiquities Scheme

Anni Byard

AMBERLEY

In memory of my friend and colleague David Wynn Williams.

First published 2019

Amberley Publishing
The Hill, Stroud
Gloucestershire, GL5 4EP

www.amberley-books.com

Copyright © Anni Byard, 2019

The right of Anni Byard to be identified as the
Author of this work has been asserted in accordance
with the Copyrights, Designs and Patents Act 1988.

ISBN 978 1 4456 7500 8 (print)
ISBN 978 1 4456 7501 5 (ebook)

All rights reserved. No part of this book may be
reprinted or reproduced or utilised in any form
or by any electronic, mechanical or other means,
now known or hereafter invented, including
photocopying and recording, or in any information
storage or retrieval system, without the permission
in writing from the Publishers.

British Library Cataloguing in Publication Data.
A catalogue record for this book is available from
the British Library.

Typeset in 10pt on 13pt Celeste.
Origination by Amberley Publishing.
Printed in the UK.

Contents

Acknowledgements

Since 2004 the post of Finds Liaison Officer (FLO) has at various times been hosted by Reading Borough Council, West Berkshire Council and Oxfordshire County Council. The post was split in 2008, with West Berkshire (and Oxfordshire) covered by the author and, since 2010, East Berkshire by the late David Williams FSA. The post has been reunified following a generous donation by Graham and Joanna Barker and since late 2018 Berkshire has had its own FLO.

David Williams and I intended to write this book together. His untimely death in December 2017 not only left a huge hole in the PAS family, but also resulted in production challenges with this book, notwithstanding the sorrow of having to write it without David. I hope I have done him justice with the finds I chose to include; we had spoken about a few that feature but the majority are my choice alone. David was a very talented archaeological illustrator but finding copies of his wonderful illustrations of artefacts has proved difficult. I am very grateful to David's cousin, Marged Haycock, for giving me permission to reproduce the illustrations I could access, and to Mike Hayworth at the Council for British Archaeology for allowing me to copy illustrations from David's book on stirrup mounts. Thank you also to Tony Howe, David's line manager at Surrey County Council, for his support and for sourcing illustrations drawn by David.

This book would not have been possible were it not for the metal detectorists and other members of the public offering their finds for recording, many of whom have done so for years and encourage others to follow best practice and record their finds. By reporting their finds it is the public who are are changing what we knew about ancient Berkshire, and ancient Britain, and ensuring that our history is recorded for future generations long after we are all gone. The Wessex Metal Detecting Club, Maidenhead Search Society and Berkshire Detectorists have all supported David and I and the Scheme over the years.

The specialism of colleagues across the profession is invaluable and I am very grateful for their support: Paul James and Sarah Orr of West Berkshire Council; Ruth Howard, Janine Fox and the staff at West Berkshire Museum in Newbury; and Fiona Macdonald and Teresa Hocking at Berkshire Archaeology in Reading. Colleagues across the PAS are always an invaluable source of support and knowledge. At the British Museum I would like to thank Michael Lewis, Claire Costin and Ian Richardson and the rest of the Central

Unit team. The National Finds Advisors provide a vital service with very limited time and resources: Kevin Leahy, Sally Worrell, Sam Moorhead, Andrew Brown and John Naylor, and to all my FLO colleagues in surrounding counties and further afield, thanks for your continued support and friendship. Without the support and enthusiasm of PAS volunteers it would be near impossible to record all the finds offered for recording: thank you to Rod Trevaskus, Margaret Bloomfield, Lindsey Smith and Michael Byard. Thanks to Lindsay Bedford, Richard Miller and the Boxford History Project for allowing me to use the images of the Boxford mosaic. Thank you also to Paul Otter for his unwavering support and humour, to Pamela Willis of the Museum of the Order of St John, to John Perkins for comments on the draft and to Connor Stait and Amberley Publishing.

Some of the descriptions of the fifty finds are based on database records written by colleagues; they are credited in the database records but are thanked again here without being individually named. Most of the images of finds are from the PAS and partner organisations and are reproduced under Creative Commons licensing (www.creativecommons.org/licensing). Others images are freely available from Wikimedia Commons. A number of images have been produced by others and these people are credited in the captions. Every attempt has been made to obtain permission for copyrighted material used in this book; however, if I have inadvertently used copyrighted material without permission or acknowledgement I apologise and will make the necessary corrections at the first opportunity. As is usual, any other errors are my own.

Anni Byard

Foreword

The places in which we live and work have a long past, but one that is not always obvious in the landscape around us. This is a forgotten past. Most of us know little about the people who once lived in our communities fifty years ago, let alone 500, or even 5,000 years past. Like us, they lived, played and worked here, in this place, but we know almost nothing of them.

History books tell us about royalty, aristocrats and important churchmen, but most others are forgotten by time. The only evidence for many of these people is the objects that they left behind, sometimes buried on purpose, but more often than not lost by chance. Occasionally, through archaeological fieldwork, we can place these objects in a context that allows us to better understand the past, but nowadays excavation is mostly development led, so only takes place when a new building, road or service pipe is being constructed.

A unique way of understanding the past is through the finds recorded through the Portable Antiquities Scheme, of which those chosen here by Anni Byard (Oxfordshire Finds Liaison Officer) are just fifty of almost 10,000 from Berkshire on its database (www.finds.org.uk). These finds were all discovered by the public, most by metal-detector users, searching in places archaeologists are unlikely to go or otherwise excavate. As such they provide important clues of underlying archaeology that (once recorded) help archaeologists understand our past – a past of the people, found by the people.

Some of these finds are truly magnificent, others less imposing. Yet, like pieces in a jigsaw puzzle they are often meaningless alone, but once placed together paint a picture. These finds therefore allow us to understand the story of people who once lived here, in Berkshire.

Dr Michael Lewis
Head of Portable Antiquities & Treasure
British Museum

Introduction

Since its inception in 1997, the Portable Antiquities Scheme (PAS) has recorded around 1.3 million objects from England and Wales, all of which have been found by members of the public. Most of these artefacts have been found by metal-detector users, but gardeners and walkers have also contributed to the Scheme. Artefacts are recorded on the freely accessible PAS website (www.finds.org.uk/database). The data is used by both amateur and professional researchers, university students, academics, metal detectorists, local history groups and schools to illustrate the history curriculum.

The PAS works through a network of Finds Liaison Officers (FLOs) who regularly attend metal-detecting club meetings and hold museum drop-in surgeries, where finders of archaeological artefacts over 300 years old can submit their finds for identification and recording.

Once recorded the objects are then returned to the finder. The alpha-numeric references (i.e. BERK-83AC41) is the find's unique code and is searchable on the PAS website. Findspots information is restricted to a 1 km square on publically accessible records to protect the landowners and the 'site', although much of what is recorded is evidence of background activity and is recovered from ploughsoil. Recording is voluntary apart from certain classes of objects which are covered under the Treasure Act 1996, for which all qualifying discoveries must be reported to the coroner within fourteen days. Currently there are

David Williams examining finds.

several criteria for what constitutes 'Treasure': any object over 300 years old that contains more than 10 per cent precious metal (gold or silver) by weight; objects of prehistoric date (i.e. pre-Roman) would be treasure if any part of it contains precious metal, or if there are two or more copper alloy (i.e. bronze) objects from the same findspot. Coins are different: a single gold or silver coin over 300 years old would not be considered treasure (and we encourage finders to report these single finds), whereas two or more gold or silver coins, or over ten copper alloy coins from the same findspot could be considered treasure and require reporting. The Treasure Act 1996 is currently under review and criteria may change in future. The old law of 'Treasure Trove' now mostly concerns precious metal finds under 300 years old hidden with the intention of recovery. The FLOs and the PAS facilitate and administer the Treasure Act on behalf of the government. Any individual can report treasure to the coroner but most finders report their objects to the FLO, who then reports to the coroner on the finder's behalf. More information about Treasure can be found on the PAS website (www.finds.org.uk/treasure) or by contacting the local Finds Liaison Officer.

The recording of artefacts has transformed our knowledge and understanding of the people that inhabited our local and national landscape in the past. Certain objects may identify a local tribe, provide evidence of cross-channel trade, show a social status or highlight religious practices and beliefs. Looking at whole artefact assemblages can literally transform the known archaeology of an area overnight.

Sadly there are people who use metal detectors for illegal purposes, to 'raid' sites – often at night, but increasingly during daylight hours – in an attempt to recover artefacts to sell illegally, which is sadly all too easy to do. This practice is known as 'nighthawking'. It is against the law to metal detect on protected archaeological sites (Scheduled Monuments), Sites of Special Scientific Interest (SSSIs) and some other designated areas. One must always have permission to detect – every single piece of land is owned by someone, even the local park. By detecting on land without permission one could be charged with trespass, criminal damage and theft, face an unlimited fine and spend up to three months in prison. The PAS works with the police, Historic England and landowners to gather evidence of nighthawking and other illegal activities related to metal detecting. Because of the trust built between bona fide detectorists and the PAS over the past twenty years it is often other detector users themselves who report illegal or suspicious activity.

Keen members of the Wessex Metal Detecting Club. (Image © Russel Garman, reproduced with kind permission)

By working together and encouraging others to report their archaeological finds we can better understand our past. Recording allows members of the public to contribute to the knowledge of our shared heritage, to contribute to history.

A newly discovered medieval coin. (Image © Russel Garman, reproduced with kind permission)

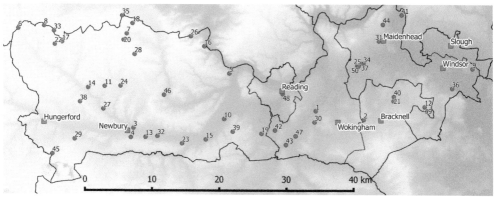

Map of Berkshire, showing the location of the fifty finds in this book.

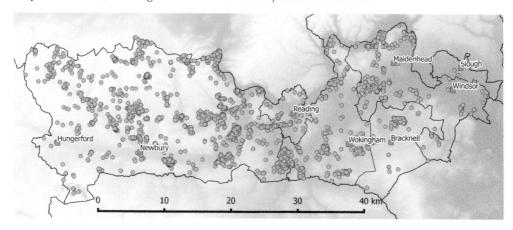

Map of all PAS finds from Berkshire.

The Berkshire Landscape

Berkshire lies in central southern England and shares borders with Oxfordshire, Buckinghamshire, Greater London, Surrey, Hampshire and Wiltshire. First recorded as a county in the late ninth century AD, the ceremonial Royal County of Berkshire now exists as six separate unitary authorities: Reading, Wokingham, Slough, Bracknell Forest, Windsor and Maidenhead and West Berkshire. The borders have changed over the years, with the greatest recent changes coming in 1974 with the loss of land to the north to Oxfordshire (now the Vale of the White Horse and parts of South Oxfordshire), and the gaining of places like Eton, Burnham and Slough. In 1995 Colnbrook and Poyle also became part of Berkshire. Taken as a whole, the current county of Berkshire covers approximately 487 square miles (1,262 square km).

Geologically the county has two main strata: nearly all of the northern edge of the county, and much of West Berkshire, lies on chalk with outcrops of clay-with-flints, while a band of London clay and associated river terrace deposits runs north-east to south-west between Slough and Bracknell, south of Reading to Thatcham. The extreme south of the county below Bracknell and areas to the south of Newbury lie on the Bagshot Formation of sands and clays. These geological strata influence the topography, soil type and ultimately the character of the landscape, both natural and man-made.

The eastern side of the county is dominated by the River Thames, which forms much of the northern border as far west as Streatley. The Berkshire Downs, part of the North Wessex Downs Area of Outstanding Natural Beauty, encompasses most of West Berkshire and then forms the border westwards, incorporating sections of the Ridgeway ancient track. Through the centre of the county from west to east runs the River Kennet, a major tributary of the Thames, which is in turn fed by the rivers Lambourn and Enbourne. Most of the rivers and streams in Berkshire eventually run into the Thames. The eastern side of the county boasts several large settlements, including the towns of Reading, Maidenhead, Slough, Bracknell and Wokingham. Due to the built-up nature of the eastern side of the county, the majority of artefacts offered for recording come from the more open, arable lands on the western side, across West Berkshire.

Looking north over the Kennet Valley from Combe Gibbet, with the North Berkshire Downs in the distance. (Image © Joolz. CC-BY-SA-2.0)

View over the Thames at Cookham Reach. (Image © Colin Smith. CC-BY-SA-2.0)

Chapter 1
The Stone Age
(700,000 – 2,400 BC)

The use of stone tools was the predominant technology of early prehistory. In Britain the period covers nearly 700,000 years and is split into three main periods: the Palaeolithic, Mesolithic and Neolithic. The Palaeolithic (Old Stone Age) is divided in to three phases due to the amount of time it covers: the Lower Palaeolithic (the earliest period, *c.* 800,000 – 150,000 BC), Middle Palaeolithic (*c.* 150,000 – 40,000 BC) and Upper Palaeolithic (*c.* 40,000 – 8,300 BC). Very generally these divisions are based on changing climatic and environmental factors, and archaeologically it represents changing technologies in stone tool manufacture.

The Palaeolithic landscape would have been almost unrecognisable to modern eyes. The climate varied from very cold glacial episodes with artic temperatures to warmer periods (interglacials). When not covered in vast ice sheets the landscape was mostly grassland with few trees. Large animals such as mammoths, elk and woolly rhinoceros roamed the land. Britain was connected to mainland Europe by a land bridge which enabled animals and early humans (*Homo antecessor* and *Homo heidelbergensis*) to visit periodically. Early human occupation would have been limited to the warmer periods. Neanderthals (*Homo neanderthalensis*) first came to Britain around 60,000 BC and modern humans (*Homo sapiens*) after 40,000 BC. Occupation didn't become permanent until after the last Ice Age, around 12,000 years ago, when temperatures slowly began to rise, resulting in changes in flora and fauna, including the expansion of woodland and a wider variety of animal and plant resources to exploit. Rising sea levels separated Britain from mainland Europe around 6,000 BC, creating the island we live on today.

Berkshire has yielded many artefacts and indeed sites of early prehistoric date. Old river channels and gravels of the Thames and especially the Kennet Valley are renowned for their Upper Palaeolithic and Mesolithic sites. Some of the earliest objects recorded with the PAS are Lower Palaeolithic flint hand axes and there are six recorded from Berkshire, including this beautiful example from Earley, which was found during weir works on the River Lodden. As the name suggests this tool was made to be used in the hand and was not hafted into a wooden or bone handle. They could have been used for a variety of uses, including butchery. The hand axe is heart-shaped (cordate) with a rounded butt and sharply tapering sides. The extreme tip of the axe is now missing. The hand axe has been bifacially worked, initially with a hard hammer (another stone) to create a rough-out and then 'thinning' flakes were removed with a soft hammer (antler or bone) to create the final size and shape. The flint has patinated an orange/ochre colour but in areas of damage the underlying flint is a light grey colour. This suggests that the initial source of the flint may have been chalk downland and the orange patination suggests the object spent a long time in the river gravels, having been deposited in its final situation by glacial or river terrace action, not necessarily far from its original site of deposition. Characteristic of the Acheulian industry of the Lower Palaeolithic, depending on which gravel terrace it originated from, this hand axe dates from *c.* 340,000 – 300,000 BC or 245,000 – 190,000 BC.

Lower Palaeolithic hand axe from Earley. 147 mm long, 91 mm wide.

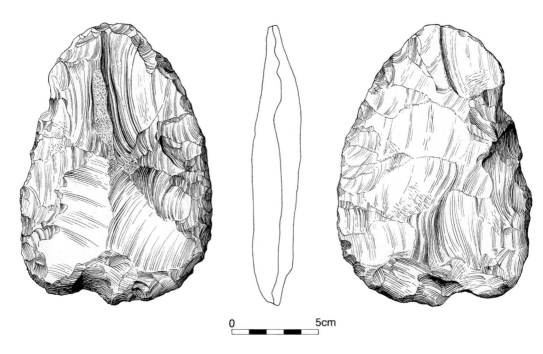

0   5cm

Above: Lower Palaeolithic hand axe from Pangbourne, found in the Thames by a police diver (BERK-71FD63). Evidence from the Lower Thames Valley suggests this type of axe belongs to the later part of the Middle Acheulian Culture. 161 mm long, 113 mm wide. (Artist unknown; on behalf of West Berkshire Council)

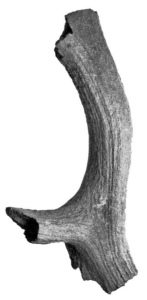

Left: A large fragment of Red Deer antler from Sulhampstead, probably Palaeolithic in date (BERK-BA3A04). Antler like this was used as a soft hammer tool in flint knapping, although there are no tool marks or signs of use on this example. 270.3 mm long, weight 481 grams.

'Penknife' points are rare finds, especially for central and south-east England. They are a diagnostic tool type and can be closely dated to the very end of the Upper Palaeolithic period, around 12,000 – 11,000 BC. Similar to points in German assemblages of the same date, the penknife point is made from a struck blade with the proximal tip (lowermost in the image) missing. The point has secondary soft hammer retouch on one long side and on the short oblique edge which forms the point. A small patch of cortex remains in the centre of the dorsal surface. These tools may have been used as projectile points for hunting game. This is the only penknife point recorded on the PAS database. It was found during a fieldwalking exercise.

The iron-stained flint blade was found in a garden in Cold Ash near Newbury and dates to the very end of the Palaeolithic period (11,000 – 8,300 BC), some 300,000 years after the hand axe illustrated opposite. Retouching is evident along both left and right dorsal edges and was probably created using a soft hammer. There is modern machine damage (plough damage) evident on both sides and the central ridge is crushed.

Above left: Penknife point from Binfield. 40.6 mm long, 13.2 mm wide.

Above right: Flint blade from Cold Ash (BERK-E568A4). 93.2 mm long, 37 mm wide.

During the Mesolithic period (Middle Stone Age) the climate warmed and the landscape was one of extensive woodlands and related flora and fauna, such as beaver, deer and pig. Although humans were generally nomadic at this point in time, there is evidence for 'base camps' as well as small rest or hunting camps. A probable base camp excavated at Thatcham produced over 18,000 flints. The assemblage included adzes and axes, scrapers and piercers and blade and bladelet waste flakes, showing that manufacturing was taking place on some scale. Although axes are still common tools, small, sometimes tiny blades called microliths are characteristic of the Mesolithic and reflect the change in available fauna from large to small game and fish. Microliths can be very difficult to spot, especially if the area is already rich with flint. However once located, they are easily identified.

Homeowner and gardener Raymond Carter had a keen interest in archaeology. During the mid to late twentieth century Raymond collected over 200 flints from his garden in Skillings Road, Newbury. The flints are evidence for Mesolithic tool manufacture and consist of mainly blade and bladelet flakes and debitage (the waste material from tool manufacture). Within the assemblage are diagnostic microliths, very small flint tools that were hafted into wood or bone using tree resin as glue. These composite tools could be used in both hunting and gathering activities.

The assemblage has several types of microlith present including oblique points, curved-backed pieces, a microdenticulate and a rare straight-backed piece (OXON-AC822D). The straight-backed point is made on a secondary flake of a semi-translucent, light-brown flint. The point has concaved basal retouch, some very fine retouch on the right lateral edge and covering retouch along the straight back. The point is still very sharp.

Left: Part of the Skillings Road assemblage. Sizes vary from 12.5 mm to 57 mm in length.

Right: Straight-backed point (OXON-AC822D). 36 mm long.

This complete flint tranchet adze was found in a garden in Newbury. The adze is made from a flint nodule and is broadly sub-rectangular in plan with both the butt end and the bladed cutting edge being slightly rounded; the adze tapers slowly from the butt end towards the blade. In section the adze is a pointed ovoid, with both butt and blade tapering in profile. The dorsal (upper) side has a high, off-centre longitudinal ridge, bevelled to each side due to flakes having been removed with a hard hammer in multiple directions. The ventral side (the underside) of the adze also has an off-centre longitudinal ridge but this is not as high nor pronounced as the dorsal ridge. At the blade end is the characteristic 'tranchet' flake removal, which gives this type of adze or pick its name. The tranchet flake was created by striking across the tip of the pick, removing a sharpening flake to create the sharp cutting edge. This object is a type used throughout the period. It would have been hafted into a wooden or bone handle and would have been used as a carpentry tool rather than for cutting down trees.

Tranchet adze from Newbury. 138.6 mm long, 43 mm wide.

Adzes like this one from the Thames at Reading may have been used for digging (SUR-C76133). They are often erroneously termed 'Thames picks' because of their discovery location. 154 mm long, 51.5 mm wide.

The Neolithic saw a change in human behaviour; the advent of widespread sedentism. Settled communities began growing crops and practised animal husbandry alongside hunting and gathering. Large areas of woodland were cleared to make way for farming and habitation. For the first time ritual and funerary monuments like stone circles, burial mounds and causewayed enclosures are seen and there are a good number of monuments within Berkshire; for example the long barrow at Combe Gibbet, cursus at Sonning and Buscot and the recently discovered causewayed enclosure near Dachet. In 2013 the remains of four Neolithic houses were discovered at Kingsmead Quarry near Horton, with radiocarbon results dating one of the houses to 3,800 – 3,640 BC, making it one of the oldest houses ever discovered in Britain. Pottery developed for the first time during the Neolithic and flint tools were adapted to reflect the changes in lifestyle. Purpose-specific tools became the norm. Arguably, flint tools are at their most aesthetic during this period.

Found at Pangbourne, this is a relatively unusual find dating from the early Neolithic period. Known as a laurel leaf point, it is made from a grey-brown flint now mottled to a light grey. Lithics of this form have an unknown function but are sometimes suggested to be rough-outs for leaf-shaped arrowheads or possibly knives. Whatever the intended final function of this object, it appears to be unfinished; the removals are large and crude, very unlike finished examples of knives or arrowheads. The flint has a sharp point and there is modern damage to the butt. This example does not display the invasive retouch along one edge that would be expected if it were to function as a knife, nor is there bifacial retouch all over the object if it were a finished arrowhead.

Laurel leaf point from Pangbourne. 67.8 mm long, 36.8 mm wide.

Neolithic 'slug' knife showing retouch along all edges. From Sunningwell and Ascot (SUR-E41676). 54 mm long.

A leaf-shaped arrowhead showing invasive retouch on each face. Found at Letcombe Regis, Oxfordshire (BERK-6C1C10). 30 mm long.

Reconstruction Neolithic longhouse at Buster Ancient Farm, Hampshire. (Image © Rob Farrow, CC-BY-SA/2.0)

This stone axe head is made from an igneous low silica rock, in terms of grain size somewhere between gabbro and coarse-grained dolorite, both of which are similar in composition to basalt. There are no natural sources of either rock in the Berkshire area; gabbro is found off the western Scottish mainland while parts of Ireland and a swathe of land from the English Midlands northwards, including the Isle of Man, have sources of dolorite. Therefore this axe head is an import into the region, probably coming through a trade network as a prestige item. The trade in finished and unfinished axe heads extended across the country and the near continent; it is the first evidence that we have in the UK for trade and commerce, and it was undertaken on an industrial scale.

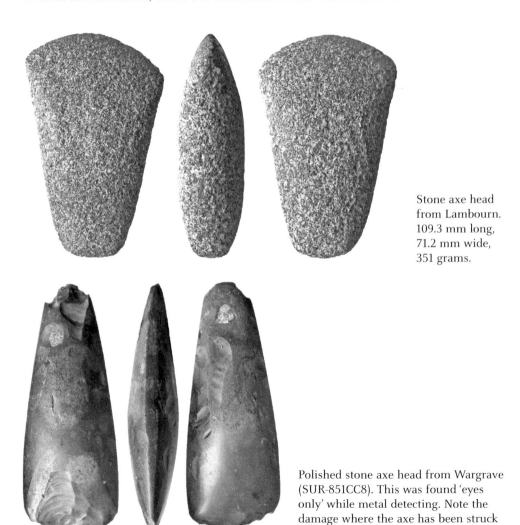

Stone axe head from Lambourn. 109.3 mm long, 71.2 mm wide, 351 grams.

Polished stone axe head from Wargrave (SUR-851CC8). This was found 'eyes only' while metal detecting. Note the damage where the axe has been struck by the plough. 167 mm long.

Chapter 2
The Bronze Age
(*c.* 2,400 – 800 BC)

Bronze is an alloy of copper and tin (*c.* 90 per cent and 10 per cent respectively). In Britain copper ores can be found in Devon, Cornwall, north Wales, west Scotland and south-west Ireland. Tin ores are located mainly in south-west Britain. Some of the earliest objects in bronze display a direct progression from flint tools. Flint continues to be used for objects like arrowheads but the quality declines and by *c.* 1,500 BC most objects that were once made in stone are now made in bronze. Many Bronze Age objects are found incomplete – they may have been discarded after they were damaged through use but as bronze was a precious and prestigious commodity, much of it would have been melted down for reuse. The presence of both complete and fragmentary objects as well as casting waste in founders' hoards attests to this practice. West Berkshire Museum's recent 'Hoards' exhibition displayed a number of collections from the Bronze Age and later periods, including examples of artefacts featured below.

West Berkshire Museum's 'Hoard' exhibition, featuring prehistoric hoards. (Produced with kind permission)

Find 7: Flat axe from West Ilsely (NMGW-901FF1)
Early Bronze Age (1,950 – 1,750 BC)

The first metal axes in Britain were made of copper rather than the alloy of bronze, having a dull red colour with a blackish patina (tarnish). This flat axe from West Ilsely is of a type known as the 'developed' flat axe, meaning that its form has developed beyond the 'simple' flat axes of the earliest Bronze Age (*c.* 2,300 – 2,050 BC), which copied flint and stone examples. Developed flat axes come in a variety of different shapes. The West Ilsley axe has raised outer edges (flanges) and an expanded crescentic blade. Axes become more technologically complex as the Bronze Age progresses, possibly related to the development of the wooden handles they were inserted into. These progressions are relatively closely datable as they are often found alongside other chronologically and typologically distinctive artefacts, often as part of hoards. This example probably falls within the late Aylesford to Willerby metalworking phases, dating from c. 1950 – 1750 BC.

Above left: Developed flat axe from West Ilsley. 101 mm long, 50.7 mm wide.

Above right: Incomplete early (undeveloped) flat axe from Swallowfield (SUR-25F712), without flanges, *c.* 2,350 – 2,050 BC. 114 mm long.

Find 8. The Crow Down hoard from Lambourn (BERK-83AC41)
Middle Bronze Age (1,400 – 1,200 BC)

In September 2004 a group of metal detectorists were searching land near the Ridgeway at Lambourn. One detectorist discovered an in situ hoard of two twisted arm/neck ornaments and three penannular bracelets, all of gold (BERK-6863E4; BERK-683F91; BERK-6870F5; BERK-687927). This is the most significant find of prehistoric metalwork ever made in the region. In their time these objects were very high status and would have been highly sought after. It is unclear why they were buried where they were. The area is rich in Bronze Age remains, including a group of over thirty prehistoric funerary monuments featuring the Lambourn Seven Barrows and is close to the Ridgeway ancient track along the North Berkshire Downs.

The twisted ornaments are coiled, either because they could be buried more easily or because they were worn curled around the arms. They both have twisted four-stranded wire bodies and plain folded-back terminals which expand gently towards the ends. The three bracelets are all penannular, although one has terminals that almost meet. Armlets and bracelets are both well-documented classes of ornament belonging to the Middle Bronze Age, c. 1,300 – 1,100 BC, and the associations of the two types of object represented in this hoard are well known. After discovery the artefacts were taken to the British Museum, where they underwent metal analysis to determine the constituents of the metal. Differing alloys were used throughout history and this can be used to help date objects. The analysis gave an estimate of around 82 per cent gold content for the objects, apart from the smaller armlet, which was 79 per cent gold. The suggested dating for the hoard is reinforced by the analyses, which accords well with other objects of this class and date.

As these objects are of prehistoric date and contain precious metal, the hoard qualified as Treasure under the Treasure Act 1996. After the coroner's inquest the hoard was purchased by West Berkshire Museum with help from the Art Fund, the finder and landowner each receiving 50 per cent of the value tax free. The hoard is currently on display in the West Berkshire Museum.

The Crow Down Hoard.
(Courtesy West Berkshire
Museum)

23

This coiled torc or bracelet with threaded penannular rings is paralleled by similar discoveries in Cambridgeshire and Norfolk. The hoard comprises a double-stranded, twisted gold wire torc with plain loop terminals, coiled and purposefully threaded with four double composite rings and one single ring, all of which have a C-shaped cross section. The composite rings vary between 11.4 and 16 mm in diameter, while the twisted torc has an uncoiled length of 97 mm. Studying the hoard at the British Museum, Gillian Varndell comments that:

> Composite rings have been found singly, linked together and associated with other gold personal ornaments. They are also found in Ireland and France, though they appear to be rarer in Ireland. At Stretham Cambridgeshire six composite rings were found threaded onto a penannular bracelet while a find from North East Norfolk comprised a plain loop of thick gold wire threaded with seven composite and two simple rings.
>
> Parallels for the double-stranded ornament are in the Middle Bronze Age Beerhackett (Dorset) hoard (which included one with a twisted body as well as a plain one) and another with a twisted body from Cross near Axminster, Devon. The French and Central European double-stranded coils all have plain, untwisted bodies. The continental examples are all made on fairly slender gold wire and most have been soldered at the ends to create loops; scientific examination of the Windsor example revealed the presence of solder on both the twisted ornaments and the rings.

The hoard was declared Treasure by the Berkshire coroner and was acquired by Windsor & Royal Borough Museum.

Gold torc and rings from
Windsor. Total weight 18.8 grams.

A growing number of gold objects of Bronze Age date are being reported from Berkshire but they are still very rare finds; to date the PAS has recorded only eight such finds from the county.

Decorated gold strip from Winterbourne (BERK-387817), *c.* 1,500 – 800 BC. 32.6 mm long.

Penannular ring from Englefield (SUSS-665261). This is a gold foil-plated copper alloy ring with silvery-gold wire inlaid into the gold foil dating from *c.* 1,150 – 800 BC. It was disclaimed as Treasure and returned to the finder. 19.2 mm diameter.

Of a type more commonly found in Ireland, this lovely spearhead is an important find. The spearhead is complete and in very good condition. It has a long sweeping blade with lunate openings and a slender, open socket. Richard Davis (University of Nottingham) comments that 'this spearhead seems to be a transitional design somewhere ... between the protected-looped, and the mature lunate spearheads typified by those from the Blackmoor [Hampshire] hoard. This would date it to the late Middle Bronze Age or early Late Bronze Age [1,100 – 900 BC].' There are no traces of wood or other organics preserved within the socket but the iron concretions suggests the spear was deposited within a wetland environment, a practice well attested in Bronze Age Britain. During this period weapons, tools and personal items were deposited in wet places, such as rivers and lakes, either complete (like this example) or in pieces, being 'ritually killed'. Fragments of lunate spearheads have been found in hoards in Ireland and recently in Wales. The Ufton Nervet spear is a rare find for southern England, not just because of its near-perfect condition.

Lunate spearhead from Ufton Nervet. 203 mm long, 59 mm wide. Socket diameter 27 mm.

Above Left: Socketed spearhead with side loops from Tidmarsh (BERK-9C5258), *c.* 1,500 – 1,150 BC. 80.7 mm long.

Above right: Small pegged spearhead from Theale (SUR-3B2641), *c.* 1,200 – 750 BC. 106.9 mm long.

Find 11. Unidentified object from Boxford (BERK-719DA8)
Middle Bronze Age – Late Iron Age (*c.* 1,300 – 100 BC)

It is not uncommon for a FLO to be handed something that they are unfamiliar with. Fortunately colleagues often come to the rescue, but there are objects that remain an enigma to the archaeological world. This object from Boxford is an example of one such group classed as 'unidentified' because no one is quite sure of what they are! Nicknamed 'moustache' mounts because of their shape, these objects come in a variety of shapes and sizes. The Boxford 'moustache' is cast in one piece and has a swollen body which tapers towards the pointed terminals. The centre of the body is narrowed and has a uniform vertical groove running around its girth. The groove abuts a circular recess, approximately 7.3 mm in diameter. All sides of the object are decorated with alternating ridges and grooves arranged horizontally.

A number of these mounts have been recovered and recorded on the PAS database. Some are 'single' examples (probably broken mounts, more reminiscent of hedgehogs!) while others are 'doubles' like the Boxford example, the drop-shaped elements often extending downwards rather than outwards. Their function is uncertain; the circular recess at the bottom of this example (and in many of the others) suggests that they were mounted on or below something. A mount for a sword or dagger handle is the most obvious function as they seem too small and impractical for a scabbard chape, but the absence of evidence makes this theory purely conjectural. A similar object was found in the Salisbury Hoard, which has associated objects dating from the Middle Bronze Age right through to the Late Iron Age. It has been suggested they are actually of Iron Age date but this is yet to be confirmed by the excavation of a stratified example.

'Moustache' mount
from Boxford.
58.5 mm long.

Above: Small 'moustache'
mount from Hampstead
Norreys (BERK-3F46D5).
34.7 mm long.

Right: Large 'moustache' mount
from Clanfield, Oxfordshire
(HAMP-6F4C45). 72.5 mm long.

This Late Bronze Age socketed axe is of a type found in southern and south-eastern England and is known as the Meldreth type, dating from *c.* 900 – 800 BC, at the very end of the Bronze Age. These axes were probably used as modern axes are – as a tool for chopping wood and organic materials – but some may have functioned as ingots or votive offerings. The axe blade is largely worn away and a section is missing from the rim. The small loop on the side of the axe would have been used to help affix the axe head to the haft more securely (see illustration). Cast in a two-piece mould, the casting seams are largely filed away but are still visible along the sides. There are large patches of corrosion where the original surface is missing. Although not uncommon in the south of England, only three confirmed examples have been recorded by the PAS from Berkshire – this example from Winkfield and two fragments from Bray (SUR-B3D798) and Warfield (SUR-2FE4D6).

Socketed axe from Winkfield.
99 mm long.

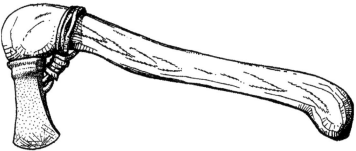

Reconstruction drawing of a Late Bronze Age socketed axe and its handle. (Illustration by David Wynn Williams, reproduced with kind permission of Marged Haycock)

Chapter 3
The Iron Age
(*c.* 800 BC – AD 43)

Like previous periods, the Iron Age is split into three phases: Early (*c.* 800 – 400 BC), Middle (*c.* 400 – 100 BC) and Late (*c.* 1 00 BC – AD 43). In Britain the Iron Age comes to an end with the Roman invasion of Emperor Claudius in AD 43. Iron Age people lived in small communities in roundhouses with enclosures, field systems and trackways linking and defining areas. They would have grown their own wheat, barley and oats and looked after animals such as sheep, cattle and pig. Large enclosures called hill forts were built from the Early Iron Age. These sites were probably used for gatherings, stock control and, if necessary, defensive purposes. As the Iron Age progresses we see a marked increase in the range of goods produced locally or imported from the Continent. A distinctive art style develops across Britain and Europe and all manner of goods and commodities, both essential and prestige items, are being traded widely.

The term 'Celt' or 'Celtic' is often used today to describe the Iron Age and its people, but it was a term used by Greek and Roman writers to describe those who lived to the west. There was no unified political identity in Britain during the Iron Age. The Atrebates, whose capital was at Calleva Atrebatum (modern Silchester, Hampshire), were the dominant tribe in the Berkshire region during the Late Iron Age, with the Dobunni to the north-west and the Catuvellauni to the north-east. A 'lost' tribe, known as the Berkshire group, are only known of through their coinage; their centre may have been at Dorchester-on-Thames (Oxfordshire) and it is likely the group was subsumed into one of the larger, more dominate tribes of the region. As more of their coins are recorded it may be possible to identify the location of manufacture, and possibly even the identity of those striking them.

Iron became the metal of choice for tools and weapons but copper alloys were still used for many personal, everyday and prestige items. Detectorists tend to discriminate against iron in their searching because of the sheer quantity of modern ironwork in the fields. Because of this bias, most of the Iron Age metalwork recorded with the PAS is of copper alloy.

Above: A replica of a typical Iron Age roundhouse, constructed in the 1980s. (Image © A. Byard, reproduced by kind permission of the Earth Trust)

Left: A Berkshire tribe 'Abingdon zoo' silver unit found at Winterbourne (BERK-92BA49) dating from *c.* 55 – 40 BC, and an interpretive illustration of a similar coin. Only around twenty of these coins are known. (Image © Philip de Jersey, reproduced with kind permission)

Find 13. Razor from Greenham (CORN-D78C78)
Early Iron Age (*c.* 700 – 600 BC)

This beautiful and complete single-edged razor is a rare find. Made of cast copper alloy, this is a 'Hallstatt' style razor (an art style or culture named after the type-site of Hallstatt in Upper Austria). The razor dates from the Lyn Fawr phase of the Early Iron Age, *c.* 700 – 600 BC. It is trapezoidal in plan with two suspension loops above a row of four inverted triangles in openwork. The crescentic blade is carefully finished and the edge is only 2 mm thick.

Several distinctive razor types are known. They are classed by trends in their appearance and named after the sites at which they were first discovered, although all razor designs are unique. The Greenham razor can be categorised as an Unterstall type, all of which have trapezoidal-shaped blades, a strengthening rib between two rings and decorative triangular perforations in the upper part of the body. They are mainly found in Western Europe in southern and central France, south-west Bavaria and northern Germany, although they have also been found further afield. Several new finds come from the southern half of England: Wickham Skeith, Suffolk; St Albans, Hertfordshire; the Salisbury/Netherhampton hoard, Wiltshire; Bowerchalke, Wiltshire; Royston, Cambridgeshire; Attleborough, Norfolk; Bicester, Oxfordshire; and this example from Greenham in West Berkshire. By finders recording their objects with the PAS, the distribution of certain artefacts can be researched alongside discoveries made through commercial and amateur archaeology projects. This allows archaeologists to place objects in their wider regional and intercontinental context; it seems plausible that these razors were being made in Britain rather than being imported.

Above left: Hallstatt razor from Greenham. 73 mm wide, 44 mm high.

Above right: Incomplete Hallstatt razor from Bishopstone, Buckinghamshire (BUC-58FFF8), *c.* 800 – 600 BC. 29.2mm long.

Right: Late Hallstatt bracelet from Steeton, North Yorkshire (YORYM-C6AAEF), *c.* 600 – 300 BC. 60.4 mm diameter.

Brooches start to be made around the fifth century BC. They could be used for a variety of purposes including securing clothing, fastening bags or just for decoration. During the Iron Age both bronze and iron brooches were made, although few iron examples survive compared to those of copper alloy. Brooch styles can be very regional; certain styles of brooch may have identified an individual as part of a certain group, as the distribution of the 'Vale' brooch type of the Berkshire/Oxfordshire area attests.

This unusual style of brooch has only recently been recognised as a regional type. Although none of these brooches have been found in datable contexts, they're likely to date from *c.* 300 – 150 BC. The Welford brooch is in the shape of a cross, made up of four circular domed knops arranged around a slightly larger central dome. Three of the domes have a hollow underside while two opposing domes are solid to support the pin and catch plate mechanism. The pin is not sprung; rather it is mounted onto a simple bar that swivels between two small protruding lugs pierced to take the bar.

This brooch is one of an increasing number of examples (nineteen at the time of writing) seemingly concentrated around the West Berkshire/Vale of the White Horse (Oxfordshire) area. Although there are several outliers, the concentration indicates a local source. Characterised by their bulbous mouldings, they appear in a variety of shapes including cross (quatrefoil around a central dome or variant – this example), square, lozengiform (with an openwork centre) and circular. Examples recorded on the PAS database from Berkshire are: BERK-9343A6, BERK-D83302, BERK-4451E9 and BERK-5F3CA5.

Middle Iron Age
'Vale' brooch
from Welford.
27.8 mm wide.

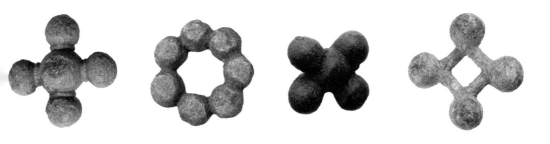

Examples of the various forms of 'Vale' brooch, clockwise from top left: BERK-4451E9, BERK-5F3CA5, WILT-BF5093, BERK-F5AF04.

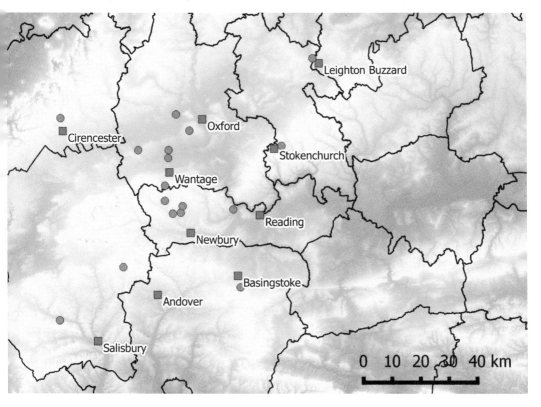

Distribution of known hollow-domed 'Vale' brooches.

A good number of Late Iron Age/Early Roman strap unions have been recorded on the PAS database and more are listed in museum collections. They come in a variety of styles and sizes, some being rather plain and utilitarian while others are highly decorative. Used to join straps on either horse harnesses or personal clothing, this well-preserved cast-copper alloy example dates to the very end of the Iron Age, and is of a type still in use into the early Roman period, *c.* 100 BC – AD 100. The fitting comprises a central body of two crescents attached point to point to form a central circular aperture. There is a circular pit in each crescent, possibly intended to take a missing stone or enamel inlay; one has been broken. On each side is a bar to take the strap and each is furnished with two pairs of double collars. The outer part of each crescent is decorated with a curving panel of engraved basketwork decoration.

Strap fitting from
Aldermaston.
27.8 mm long,
25 mm wide.

A small Late Iron Age strap
fitting from Remenham
(HAMP-5287B5).
31.5 mm high.

A highly decorative strap
fitting from Wakefield,
Yorkshire (SWYOR-6EE012).
47 mm high.

Fob danglers remain a poorly understood artefact type. They were probably associated with horse harnesses, personal adornment or possibly furniture decoration and they date from the Late Iron Age or Early Roman period. The PAS has contributed significantly to the corpus of examples from Britain, enabling further research and investigation to be conducted. Fob danglers often depict a triskele, from the Greek word meaning 'three-legged', or a variation on that theme. The spiral motif is seen in prehistoric rock art but is most commonly associated with Iron Age art. The fob dangler from Streatley is unusual as it comprises four arms rather than three, spiralling from a central hub. On the outer edge of each spiralling arm is a seated bird, possibly intended to be a duck. Each bird has a pair of recessed eye pits which may have held a decorative insert such as a coloured stone or enamel. The upper side of the object is extensively decorated with punched rings and dots and groups of pits. At the root of each arm is a group of three rings and dots arranged in a triangle. There is a further ring and dot on the centre of each arm and a fifth at each rounded terminal. Further small punched pits adorn other areas of the fob. The underside is plain and undecorated. This appears to be the first recorded example of a fob dangler with bird terminals. Such is its uniqueness that the object was kindly donated by its finder to West Berkshire Museum.

Above left: Fob dangler strap fitting from Streatley. 57 mm diameter.

Above right: More common style of 'fob dangler' with three arms and suspension loop from Bampton, Oxfordshire (BH-33103E). 21 mm high, 21 mm diameter.

This figurine shares characteristics with examples from the Continent as well as several heads and busts from Late Iron Age Britain. Nearly complete, this copper alloy anthropomorphic figurine is crudely cast. It probably depicts a male although no genitalia is evident. The figure is standing with its arms raised slightly from the sides, although one arm is missing, as is one foot. Compared to the rest of the figure the head is well cast, with eyes, nose and mouth clearly depicted. The figure wears either a helmet with linear decoration or, more likely, the mouldings represents the hair, which sits flat across the brow and tapers to a point at the base of the neck and towards the location of the ears (which are not depicted). The rest of the figurine is almost flat with no body features portrayed. The surviving right arm terminates in a loop – presumably the figure held something like a rod through its hand, but like the rest of the body there is no anatomic detail. The body of the figure is very long – there is a widening and then tapering of the central section of the figure, probably indicating a waist. This may suggest that the figure is wearing a long, knee-length robe. The legs and right foot remain intact, and again there is no detail on either.

Above left: Human figurine from East Garston. 52.5 mm high, 27.9 mm wide.

Above right: Anthropomorphic pin head from Itchen Valley, Hampshire (HAMP-997D86). 12.9 mm high.

The earliest single find of a Roman silver coin in Britain was found by Malcolm Langford near the ancient Ridgeway trackway. The coin was minted in Rome between 211 and 207 BC, when Rome was a Republic.

Although Republican denarii are not particularly uncommon finds, when they are found they are often much worn. Denarii remained in circulation for a long time because of their bullion value. When found in a hoard they are often associated with much later Roman coins and this is why this coin is special – it was an isolated find and its condition suggests that it wasn't in circulation for long before it was lost. Coinage didn't arrive in Britain until the mid-second century BC. The small amounts that did circulate would have arrived in Britain through cross-channel trade, immigrant settlers and returning mercenaries. It is likely that this coin was lost sometime during the first century BC. The head of Roma can be seen on the obverse while the reverse depicts the galloping Dioscuri, twin half-brothers Castor and Pollux, considered to be semi-divine in Roman Mythology. Legend has it that the Dioscuri fought for Rome in the first battle for the Republic, 12 miles south-east of Rome at Lake Regillus in *c.* 496 BC. They miraculously appeared in the forum at Rome to inform the city of the win immediately after the battle ended, and disappeared once they had delivered the news.

Roman Republican denarius from West Ilsley. 18.5 mm diameter.

Classical statues of
Castor and Pollux
on the Capitoline
Hill, Rome.

The author, Sir Tony
Robinson and finder
Malcolm Langford
discussing the coin on
Channel 4's *Ancient
Tracks.* (Courtesy of
Doubleband Films)

Towards the end of the first century BC, local tribes began minting their own coinage, much of it based on Continental (especially Greek and Roman) designs, although more abstract. The use of coins would have been restricted to those with a standing in society; for most people commerce would have revolved around the trade and exchange of goods and services rather than a monetary system. Known to numismatists as 'staters' (we don't know what the Iron Age people called them), a small hoard of eight Late Iron Age gold coins was found by four detectorists near Wokefield. The coins are all of the same type (sometimes called the Selsey two-faced type) and were issued by the local Regini and Atrebates tribe between *c.* 60 and 20 BC. The obverse ('head' side) has an abstract interpretation of a laureate head facing right while the reverse depicts a triple-tailed horse advancing right with a charioteer's arm above and a wheel below. These coins have a dished or concaved profile and the designs are frequently struck off-flan, as examples are in this hoard. After being declared Treasure and the finders rewarded, the coins were acquired by West Berkshire Museum, where they are on display.

Iron Age coin hoard from Wokefield (obverse/reverse). The coins average 19 mm diameter.

Two shekel coin of Carthage struck in the region of Zeugitana (264 – 241 BC). British coins may be based on designs seen on coins like this.

Chapter 4
The Roman Period (AD 43 – 409)

Emperor Claudius successfully invaded Britain in AD 43, meeting little resistance when he landed on the south-east coast. After winning a large battle against the British tribes near Rochester, the Romans pushed west and northwards and were able to bring much of Britain under Roman military control within four decades. Local tribal chiefs found themselves inferior to a foreign power and many had to eventually accept Roman rule; Boudicca is the most famous exception to this. Archaeological research has shown that for the vast majority of Britons daily life continued much as it always had, with exposure to Roman goods and lifestyles taking many years to infiltrate all parts of the country. The arrival of the Romans brought an influx of people with new goods, new styles of dress and architecture and their exotic gods. These Roman gods could be paralleled with local pagan deities; both the Romans and the native people adapted and amalgamated their gods. Objects with Christian symbolism begin to appear in the late fourth century but polytheism remained the dominant belief system until the seventh century AD.

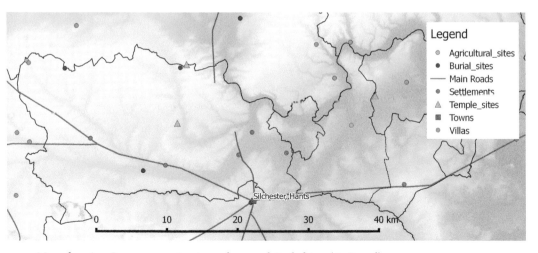

Map showing Roman remains in and around Berkshire. (A. Byard)

Around Berkshire, the Late Iron Age tribal centre of the Atrebates, Calleva (near modern Silchester), became a large and important Roman town (Calleva Atrebatum). Much of the massive town wall, built in the third century AD, still stands today.

Berkshire boasts Roman roads, temples, rural settlements and villas. Recent excavations at Boxford uncovered a villa with a fantastically preserved mosaic depicting scenes from Greek mythology.

The range of non-ferrous objects both imported and made in Britain during the Roman period is extensive. In copper alloys there are coins, brooches, finger rings, furniture fittings, cart fittings, personal hygiene and medical implements, religious and iconographic statues and figurines, belt buckles, spoons and pans, to name but a few. As well as being used in coinage, the more precious metals of silver and gold were used to produce more expensive items of personal adornment.

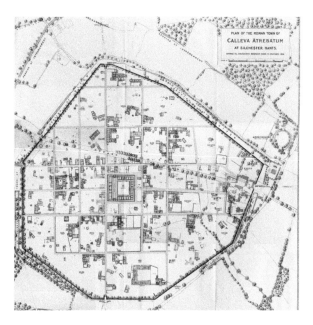

Above left: 1903 plan of Calleva Atrebatum (Silchester).

Above right: The south-east wall of Calleva Atrebatum. (Image © Edmund Shaw. CC-BY-SA/2.0)

The Boxford mosaic (Image © Richard Miller, reproduced with kind permission)

This beautifully cast eagle's head is one of a growing number of cart fittings to have been identified and recorded. Although incomplete, the eagle's head is beautifully rendered with feathers delineated both by moulding and incisions. The eye is moulded with a punch for the pupil and the eagle grasps a spherical object in its open beak. The head emerges from a sleeve consisting of three petals, a feature that is present but variable on all known examples. The sleeve would have continued for several centimetres.

The West Ilsley fitting has an iron tang within the sleeve affixed with lead – this is probably part of the cart feature onto which the fitting was mounted. These objects tend to be identified as mounts to which the reins were tied when the vehicle was stationary. Examples where the body element is complete suggest that the socket would have had a hooked projection, usually described as a swan's head, to help secure and tie-off the reins. The eagle (Aquila) was an important symbol to the military; each legion had its own Aquila standard. The tie-off projections could be interpreted as swans or geese; the coupling of an eagle (symbol of the military and also of Jupiter, the Roman's chief god) and a swan (another symbol of Jupiter) seems perfectly reasonable. The goose is a symbol of Juno (Jupiter's wife and protector of the Roman senate and people); thus, a goose would symbolise the union of two of Rome's principal deities, the prowess of the army, the senate and of Roman rule. Their appearance may also entreaty the protection of the gods. Similar cart fittings are known from the Continent around the Danube and Rhineland regions, suggesting a military connection and a first-century AD date. Further research is required in this area but the fourteen eagle head cart fittings recorded with PAS (all from the south and east of the country) are making a large and important contribution to the corpus of these early Roman objects.

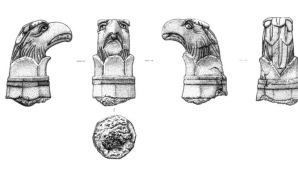
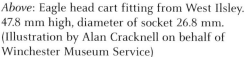

Above: Eagle head cart fitting from West Ilsley. 47.8 mm high, diameter of socket 26.8 mm. (Illustration by Alan Cracknell on behalf of Winchester Museum Service)

Right: Examples of probable goose/peacock head fittings (recorded as swan's heads) from the PAS database (BERK-A460DA, LIN-567032 and HAMP2939).

Roman coins make up the largest proportion of finds recorded by the PAS – over 300,000 individual coins at the time of writing. From Berkshire there are around 2,500 Roman coins recorded, nearly 27 per cent of all finds of all periods recorded from the county.

Struck in Rome, this silver denarius of Vespasian (ruled AD 69 –79) is in fantastic condition. The reverse depicts Neptune standing left, foot on the prow of a boat, with a dolphin and trident. The inscription COS ITER TR POT are abbreviations of his political titles: COS (consulship), ITER (meaning 'again', referring to his second consulship), TR POT (*Tribunicia Potestas*) tribune of the people). This combination of titles allows us to date the coin to AD 70. Vespasian brought stability and security to Rome after a series of civil wars that resulted in four emperors in one year (the previous three, Galba, Otho and Vitellius, all met untimely deaths). Vespasian secured Roman rule over Britain and Germany but is most famous for the construction of the Colosseum.

Denarius of Vespasian from Warfield. 18.9 mm diameter.

This copper alloy sestertius of Emperor Trajan is a rare coin, and being only slightly worn makes it even more appealing. Struck in Rome between AD 112 and 114, the reverse depicts the entrance to Trajan's Basilica Ulpia in Rome showing three bays, each of a pair of columns mounted on a stepped platform with statuary located in the attic above. In the centre is a facing quadriga (four-horsed chariot) led by a pair of soldiers while on each side is a biga (two-horsed chariot) flanked by a military standard. Above the statues the roof of the basilica can be seen, with more columns in the background. The legend around the outer edge of the reverse is worn but otherwise the coin is in very good condition. The Basilica Ulpia was in the centre of Trajan's Forum in Rome and was completed *c.* AD 112. It was a grand structure designed by the emperor's architect Apollodorus and became the architectural blueprint for future public law courts and buildings. This coin commemorates its completion. The remains of the basilica can still be seen in Rome today.

Above: Sestertius of Trajan from Lambourn. 33 mm diameter.

Right: Remains of Trajan's Basilica Ulpia in Rome. Note Trajan's Column in the background. (Image © Pablo Cabezos. CC-BY-2.0)

47

This incomplete and plough-damaged sheet copper alloy vessel and associated rim may have been used as a cremation vessel and dates to the first or second century AD. The vessel is globular with an everted rim and flat base with low pedestal rim. The base shows concentric rings and a central dimple, suggesting that a lathe was used to raise the metal into a thin sheet. There is evidence for other lathe-risen metal vessels from Misbourne Valley, near Amersham (Buckinghamshire), and also on the PAS database (see SWYOR-ED47D0 and GLO-048BB1). The gash through the side of the vessel has been caused by modern ploughing, which dislodged the vessel from its original context.

Found with the damaged vessel was a substantial and highly decorative rim depicting heavily stylised birds' heads forming the spout. The serrations along the beaks (*tomia*) and the lack of the distinctively curving beaks that would indicate ibis suggests that the birds are swans or geese; the swan is seen as an embodiment of Jupiter, the Roman version of the supreme Greek god Zeus, as read in the story of Leda and the swan, while, as discussed above, the goose is sacred to the Roman goddess Juno. As identification of the birds' heads is uncertain, one cannot infer meaning or application to their appearance. Interestingly the rim is silvered and the remains of the sides below the rim does not correspond in thickness (or quality) to the damaged rim of the globular vessel. It would therefore seem plausible that we are in fact looking at two vessels, the second of which was not located by the detectorist, or alternatively the rim could have been deposited in its current condition with (or within) the vessel as an offering. No evidence for the walls and base of a second, silvered vessel was found.

Damaged cremation vessel from Brimpton. 185 mm wide, 150 mm high. (Image by Rod Trevaskus on behalf of Oxfordshire County Museum Service)

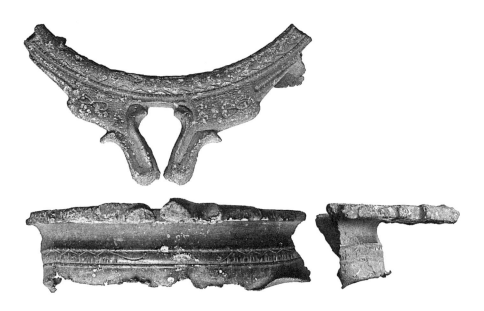

Bird's head vessel rim. 125 mm maximum width. (Image by Magdalena Wachnik on behalf of Oxfordshire County Museum Service)

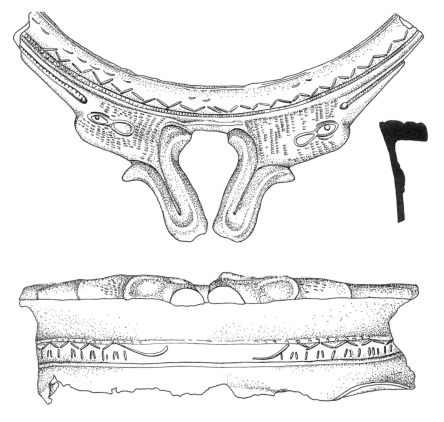

Illustration showing detail of bird's head vessel rim. (Illustration by Magdalena Wachnik on behalf of Oxfordshire County Museum Service)

This slightly damaged copper alloy figurine is probably from a small household shrine. The statue depicts a naked and chubby winged boy, a *putto*, seated with his arms around the neck of a goose. The boy's left leg is bent at the knee back towards his buttocks while the right leg is bent in front of the left knee. He sits on a round disc that acts as the base of the statue. The goose is cradled above the boy's left leg and he holds its beak under his chin; his arms grasp the goose's neck, right hand above left. The boy wears a Corinthian cap and a line of curls can be seen protruding from beneath. Two small wings, now worn and incomplete, protrude from his back below the shoulders. Although there is damage and some corrosion to the statue, the detail is still quite good; the facial features are well defined and the fingers are distinguishable. The feathers on the goose's wings are also clearly defined.

The boy's pose initially looks like he is about to wring the goose's neck, but there are many representations of *putti* playing (or struggling) with animals, the most famous of which is probably the third-century BC Hellenistic 'Boy with Goose' sculpture attributed by Pliny (N.H.xxxiv. 84) to Boethos of Chalcedon, of which in Roman times many copies were made. The style of the Winterbourne figurine indicates that it is of Romano-British manufacture and not imported (Martin Henig, University of Oxford). This type of art is termed 'genre art' as it represents an aspect of everyday life, in this case a child playing with his pet.

Above: Boy and goose figurine from Winterbourne. 60 mm high.

Left: Roman copy of Boethos' Boy and Goose sculpture, found in Rome and now on display at the Louvre, Paris.

Another example of a Roman *putto* figurine is this copper alloy example from Waltham St Lawrence. Depicting a naked child (a cupid), the figurine is in the throes of a dance, a stance often seen in such figures; the right arm is raised, the right leg is kicked back and the head is thrown skywards. Although the front of the figurine and its facial features are a little worn, the back is better preserved. The hair is held in a small bun at the neck and the details of the hair are engraved. Both of the hands and the right foot are missing. Emma Durham (University of Reading) comments that:

> The Cupid is very typical of the pieces found in Britain, the majority of which are in this stance, looking up and with the right arm raised. More generally the hair is in ringlets rather than the bun which this piece has. There are a number of Cupids like this from northern Britain, but they tend to have longer skinnier limbs and bodies. This ... is more similar to an example from Avebury or a larger statuette from Cirencester which is wingless.

The function is unknown but it was probably related to religious activity either as a votive deposit or a household god.

Dancing cherub
figurine from Waltham
St Lawrence.
61 mm high.

Other examples of
dancing figures from
the PAS (BERK-536215,
LVPL-E54C5A,
BERK-EA42E1).

Roman brooches, used to secure items of clothing or just act as decoration, come in a wide variety of forms. Some of the earliest brooches to appear in Britain look a little like safety pins, having a curved bow, spring or hinge at one end and a pin secured by a catch. From the second century more elaborate forms appear, including plate brooches of which this is a particularly unusual example. The brooch has a circular body with a central projection that terminates in a small solid disc filled with a design executed in red and white enamel. There are four rounded knops protruding from the edge of the main body of the brooch with each knop being filled with red enamel. The field of the main body is filled with a white enamel, much of which survives. Within the main field are several small rounded cells spaced equidistant around the circumference. These are now devoid of their setting but may have also contained enamel, possibly in red to continue to the theme seen on the rest of the brooch. On the reverse is the remains of the catch plate and the double-lug pin mount but the pin itself is missing. This brooch is of unusual form and is probably Continental in origin. It shares design characteristics with both flat plate brooches with peripheral lugs of British origin and 'tutulus' brooches of the second century AD.

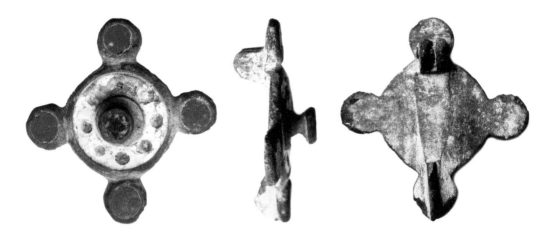

Enamelled plate brooch from Streatley. 38.3 mm long.

Lozengiform plate brooch from West Ilsley (SUR-8B98EA).

Headstud brooch from Hampstead Norreys (BERK-5B00D0).

Spoked disc brooch from Lambourn (LANCUM-254F64).

As well as being functional items of dress, brooches could also convey religious or cultural affiliation. There are several styles of brooch that can be associated with religious beliefs, such as this wonderfully preserved cockerel brooch from Boxford. With colourful wings of red and blue enamel, the three-dimensional cockerel retains the beak and comb and its tail – quite often brooches like these are damaged or broken through years of being churned around in the ploughsoil. The cockerel has two circular mouldings to represent eyes with the central cells retaining some of the red enamel that would have filled them. Beneath the eyes the wattle has a small triangular cell filled again with a red enamel. The underside of the cockerel is hollow with the remains of the pin hinge and part of the catch plate intact, but missing the pin. Cockerels (heralds of the new day) are associated with Mercury, the messenger of Jupiter. Mercury is often depicted with wings on his head and sometimes his feet, indicating his swift flight through the air. He was also protector of merchants and travellers and is one of the most frequently found deities in Roman Britain. The temple site at Uley in Gloucestershire seems to have been dedicated to him. There are a good number of objects recorded with the PAS that can be directly associated with Mercury, including anthropomorphic and zoomorphic figurines, brooches, finger rings and vessel mounts.

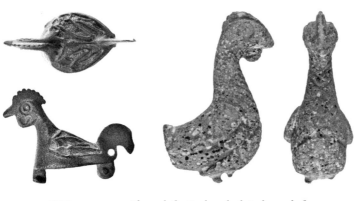

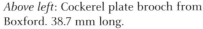

Above left: Cockerel plate brooch from Boxford. 38.7 mm long.

Above right: Cockerel figurine from Eastbury (WILT-B833B9).

Left: Figurine of Mercury from Shiplake, Oxfordshire (BERK-005B54). Note the wings on the hat and heel.

Miniature representations of tools and other objects are becoming more common thanks to detectorists recording their finds with the PAS. Axes are the most frequently found miniature objects from Roman Britain and many indicate the presence of religious complexes such as temples, shrines or sometimes graves. This tiny pair of callipers are the first of their type to be recorded, and again are likely to have had a votive use. Each arm consists of a flat, roughly circular head approximately 10.5 mm diameter with a hole for the pin close to the top edge. Measuring just 28 mm in length, the two jaws open and close freely and pivot on a 5.8 mm pin. The two claws curve like a crab claw to meet precisely. The pin is significantly wider than the two arms together, which may suggest a component is missing. Of examples recorded on the PAS database, miniature objects come in the form of axes, swords/daggers, spears, shields, hammers, razors, vessels and even miniature altar pedestals inlaid with enamel.

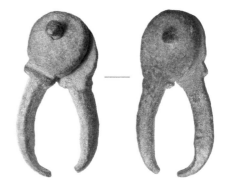

Right: Miniature callipers from Beedon.
28.3 mm long.

Below: Miniature objects from Berkshire: axe with handle from East Ilsley with possible votive markings (BERK-E93EF6), 37.4 mm tall; axe from Waltham St Lawrence (SUR-B2AC81), 28 mm long; socketed axe head from Bisham (HAMP-6EF338), 19 mm long.

55

A great many objects of lead are recovered from the fields by detectorists. Most pieces are just scrap lead while a few are recognisable objects, such as post-medieval tokens, toys and musket balls. Recognisable and indeed datable Roman lead objects are not common finds. This lead weight from Kintbury could be disregarded as 'just' an undatable weight, but it has been stamped with a Latin name. Sub-circular in plan and quite worn (lead being a soft material), one side of the weight is stamped with horizontal panels that contain the inscription QEM[..]NVS / QIMINVS (the Qs are probably Gs) – possibly giving the name of the owner or merchant as Germinus, a common name during the period (Roger Tomlin, University of Oxford, pers. comm.). The weight has then been rotated 180° and the same two individual panels stamped again. The 'S' in the inscription is reversed.

A small hole has been drilled in the reverse of the object, although the reason for this, and indeed the period in which it occurred, is unknown. This is probably a trade weight, used in conjunction with scales to weigh out goods. There are a few examples of weights inscribed or stamped with their value but this object appears to be one of the first recorded with an owner's stamp.

The Roman system of weights was similar to the imperial pound and ounces used today. There were 12 Roman ounces, or *unciae*, to the pound (*libra*); one *uncial* weighed 27.288 grams (as opposed to our imperial 28.4 grams), making a *libra* 327.45 grams (rather than our 454 grams). The Kintbury object weighs in at 148.6 grams. Paul Booth of Oxford Archaeology comments that: 'If this weight related to the Roman system ... then [it] could approximate to half a pound ... allowing for weight loss because of the hole drilled in it, and also for the fact that most recorded weights seem to fall short of the notional values (which in this case would be 163.73 g).'

Above left: Lead weight from Kintbury. 37.6 mm long, 15.7 mm thick.

Above right: Weight with inscription interpretation.

Left: Lead and iron steelyard weight from Lambourn (BERK-0ADFCD). The biconical form is typical for the Roman period.

This stunning gold solidus of emperor Valentinian I (AD 364–75) is one of only twenty recorded with the PAS of this period and the seventh of this emperor. Gold Roman coins are very rare finds. Single gold (and silver) coins do not currently qualify as Treasure and are therefore returned to the finder once they've been recorded; however, the few gold Roman coins that have been recorded are a true representation of their rarity rather than any (incorrectly) perceived issues surrounding retention of such artefacts by detectorists.

Valentinian was born in Pannonia (areas of modern-day Austria and Hungary) and was chosen to rule after the deaths of the previous emperors (by this period the empire was split into east and west, with a ruler in each province). Appointing his brother Valens to rule the Eastern Provinces, Valentinian retained the West. Valentinian spent much of his life commanding the military in the west. The reverse of this coin says 'RESTITVTOR REI PVBLICAE', meaning 'ruler of the Republic', and depicts the emperor in military attire standing with head facing right, holding a military standard with the Christian Chi-Ro symbol and a victory on a globe. Stuck in Trier (Germany), this coin dates from 25 February 364 – 24 August 367), although a more precise date of AD 364 has been suggested. Valentinian faced severe revolts in Britain, which he sent Count Theodosius (father of the future Theodosius I) to suppress. Late in AD 375, Valentinian received a deputation of barbarians and was so enraged at their impudence that he fell into an apoplectic fit and died, aged fifty-four.

Above left: Solidus of Valentinian I from Aborfield and Newland. 21.6 mm diameter.

Above right: Solidus of Valentinian II (AD 388 – 392) from Brimpton (HAMP37).

A contemporary copy of a solidus of Leo I (AD 457 – 474) from Fawley (BERK-1DEAFC). The coin is either heavily gilded copper alloy or a heavily alloyed gold.

Chapter 5
The Early Medieval Period (AD 409 – 1066)

Most of the evidence for the early part of this period comes from cemeteries (for example at East Shefford and Burghfield). We see the establishment of small farmsteads, villages and some larger settlements, including a royal palace at *Windlesora* (now Old Windsor) and a royal estate at Cookham. Early Saxon churches are known at a number of places including at Sonning, which is said to have been established by St Birinus, credited with converting local kings to Christianity in AD 636 at Dorchester on Thames.

The name Berkshire was first recorded in AD 860 as *Berrocshire*. At this time the county was on the borders of the kingdoms of Wessex and Mercia and areas of the county changed hands several times. The Danes held Reading in AD 871, the first time the town is mentioned in historical records. Æthelwulf, king of the West Saxons, beat the Danes in a battle at Englefield that same year and his brother, the future Alfred the Great, won a great battle at Ashbury, near Wantage on the Berkshire Downs. After becoming king, Alfred, born in Wantage (then Berkshire) went on to entreaty the Danes and succeeded in securing and enlarging his southern kingdom.

Soon after the Roman administration withdrew coinage ceased; a few late Roman silver coins (silique) often with clipped edges are the last of the coinage for well over 200 years. To date the PAS has recorded twenty-five silique from Berkshire. Coinage reappears around AD 700 in the form of small silver coins called sceattas. Again these are rare coins, with only around eighteen known from the county.

Finds from the period between the collapse of Roman rule and the Battle of Hastings (the early medieval period) are not particularly common in modern Berkshire, with only around 230 finds recorded on the PAS database.

Above left: Statue of Alfred the Great in his birth town of Wantage, now Oxfordshire. (Image © P. Otter)

Above right: Selection of coins and artefacts from the Watlington Hoard (Oxfordsire), excavated by David Williams. The hoard contained seven items of jewellery, fifteen silver ingots and 186 complete silver coins, mostly of Alfred the Great and Ceolwulf II of Mercia. The hoard was probably buried by a Viking for safekeeping during the 870s when Wessex and Mercia were fighting to save their kingdoms. (Image © Trustees of The British Museum/PAS)

Clipped silique of Valens (AD 364 – 378) from Streatley (SUR-28484D). 12.9 mm diameter.

Series K 'wolf' sceatta (AD 720 – 740) from Bradfield (BERK-EC0200). 11.1 mm diameter.

This extremely unusual brooch is made from cast- and gilded copper alloy and is called a wide equal-armed brooch. One sub-triangular arm, much of the arched bow and traces of the second arm are intact. The centre of the remaining arm is decorated with opposed S-scrolls with curving tendril ornament within a double linear border. Running along the base of the arm and up around the outer edges to either side of the bow are a number of quadrupeds, all biting the rump of the animal in front. The final animal has long ears and it may be a hare; depictions of hounds chasing hairs is seen on Roman knife handles. The arched bow is flattened in section with raised edges and is decorated with symmetrically opposed S-scrolls on either side.

A close parallel for this brooch was excavated at Sutton Courtenay (now in Oxfordshire) and is owned by the Ashmolean Museum. Another incomplete example was found at Berinsfield (Oxfordshire) by Oxford Archaeology. There are also parallels from Haslingfield and Little Wilbraham, both in Cambridgeshire.

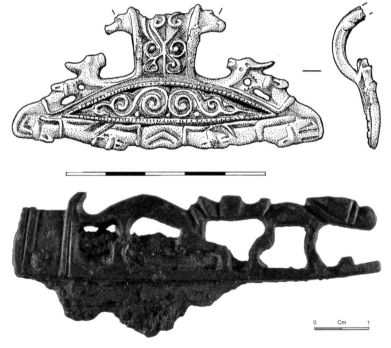

Equal-armed brooch from Maidenhead. 78 mm wide. (Illustration © David Williams, reproduced with kind permission of Marged Haycock)

Hare and hound knife handle from Liddington, Wiltshire (NMGW-A059EA). 68.4 mm long. Note the remains of the iron knife blade.

This incomplete cast-copper alloy 'crescent' buckle of late Roman/early Anglo-Saxon date is one of only five examples recorded. The buckle is broadly D-shaped in plan but has an open back where a separate iron strap bar would have been located. The strap bar was secured in place by being inserted through two small holes in the buckle frame. The frame has a flat underside and bevelled upper side, narrowing in thickness from the inside of the frame to the outer edge. Two raised V-shaped mouldings are set at a slight angle either side of the flat, undecorated pin rest. These are probably intended to be dolphin heads with open mouths, devolved from those seen on late Roman buckles; multiple recessed dots around the outer edges of the frame completes the decoration. The underside of the buckle is flat, plain and undecorated.

Stuart Laycock identified this buckle as only the fourth example of a crescent buckle at the time of discovery; these buckles form a distinct typological group with a limited geographical spread. Recently another example has been recorded from Tisbury in Wiltshire, which brings the total from that county to three, with another example coming from Oxfordshire. The buckle is typified by the separate spindle while still displaying the stylised dolphin heads seen on contemporary buckles of the fifth century AD. An example from Upper Upham, Wiltshire and now in the Ashmolean Museum is more obviously zoomorphic in design than the example recorded here; the mouldings on the Thatcham example are more devolved and abstract but bear close similarity to two other examples, from an unknown location in Berkshire and from Kelmscott, Oxfordshire. All three recent discoveries are between 25 and 27 mm long.

Crescent buckle from Thatcham. 25 mm wide.

Above: Crescent
buckle from
Tisbury, Wiltshire
(WILT-CD0A21).

Left: Late Roman
buckle from
Nether Wallop,
where the
dolphins' heads
are clearly visible
(WILT-169D92).

There are such large amounts of modern ferrous material in the fields that metal detectorists tend to set their machines to find only non-ferrous metals. As a result iron objects are not commonly offered for recording with the PAS. Their fragmentary nature, the poor condition of survival and the fact that many objects haven't changed style in hundreds of years means that when they do come in it is often difficult to assign a specific function or date to such objects. However, there are some objects that can be identified with certainty; these two Anglo-Saxon spearheads from Lambourn are examples of such. Ploughed up by a farmer in the late 1980s, they were found around 500 metres apart. Both spearheads date from the sixth or seventh century AD and they may have been grave goods. During this period men were buried with weapons such as spears, swords and shields. One of the spearheads shows corrosion (the red in the image) and is in poor condition while the other survives complete. The first spearhead (BERK-DB79D9) has a long, slender leaf-shaped blade with a long open socket into which a wooden shaft would have been inserted. The spearheads measures 540 mm in length. The second spearhead (BERK-DB89E6) is in poor condition, having suffered corrosion and damage along the blades and the socket. Measuring 400 mm in length, the spearhead has a leaf-shaped blade with a slightly raised midrib to form a flattened diamond-shaped cross section. The socket, being only around one fifth of the overall length, has probably lost its end section.

Left: The first Anglo-Saxon spearhead from Lambourn (BERK-DB79D9). 540 mm length. (Image by Rod Trevaskus on behalf of Oxfordshire County Museum Service)

Right: The second Anglo-Saxon spearhead from near Lambourn (BERK-DB89E6). 400 mm length. (Image by Rod Trevaskus on behalf of Oxfordshire County Museum Service)

Apart from a tiny number of gold coins, silver pennies were the only denomination of coin struck for a number of centuries and coins of the early Anglo-Saxon kings are not common finds. The powerful Mercian ruler Offa is one of the most famous of these kings, best known for the dyke built on his command, but even so his coinage is rare, with only around 100 coins recorded on the PAS database. Of the four examples from Berkshire, this silver penny from Shottesbrook is in the best condition. It depicts Offa facing right, in the style of a Roman emperor, wearing armour (cuirassed) with a drape over the top. The inscription reads simply 'OFFA REX' or Offa, king. As is normal on coins of this period, the reverse gives the name of the moneyer, the person responsible for the coin's striking. The letters of the moneyer's name are arranged across the petals of a quatrefoil: +P/EN/DR/Ed (Pendred), who was working at London. This coin can be dated to AD 765–92.

Offa became ruler of the House of Mercia after a period of civil war in the kingdom. During his reign he extended Mercian control and overlordship over much of England, including Wessex and Kent. In 779 Offa defeated Cynewulf, king of Wessex, at a decisive battle at Bensington, modern Benson, in Oxfordshire. Offa also took control of the royal estate at Cookham. Some of his coins and indeed some Anglo-Saxon charters (in the ninth century) refer to him as 'Bretwalda' or High King of England. After Offa's death the power and influence of the kingdom of Wessex once again increased.

Silver penny of Offa from Shottesbrook. 16.7 mm diameter.

Other Offa coins found in Berkshire: BUC-5FCC31 from Grazeley, BERK-399C86 from Great Shefford, and BUC-7AB427 from Bisham.

The longest ancient monument in Britain, Offa's Dyke, runs for 80 miles along the Welsh and English border. (Image © Chris Heaton, CC-BY-SA/2.0)

This silver zoomorphic fitting is part of a corpus of early medieval socketed zoomorphic terminals, the precise function of which is unclear. Although small, it is of fine workmanship. The mount is in the form of a possible eagle or dragon's head. Its terminal is hollow-cast with a pyramidal socket of rectangular section. This may have held a wooden rod, secured in place by the silver rivet seen through the top of the beast's head. Seen from above, the large drop-shaped eyes taper into spirals. These spirals may be intended as ears; they turn inwards and then outwards again to end in two lobes which hang down the sides of the terminal. Two very elongated nostrils are located above the muzzle; the mouth is bold, ending above what may be a protruding rolled-up tongue.

All the zoomorphic elements on the fitting are gilded, accentuating the design. Although several of these terminals are known they all vary in design, and quite possibly use. They have been described variously as decorative fittings from the tips of drinking horns and as sword scabbard mounts. Fanciful or exaggerated representations of beasts are common in Anglo-Saxon art. This example is characteristic of eighth- and ninth-century metalwork and sculpture, especially that centred on the kingdom of Mercia and its dependencies. This example probably dates to the end of the eighth century AD. As it is over 300 years old and made substantially of silver it qualified as Treasure and was acquired by West Berkshire Museum, where it is on display.

Silver mount from West Ilsley. 24.6 mm long.

In 1998 David Williams published his volume 'Late Saxon Stirrup-Strap Mounts, a Classification and Catalogue' through the Council for British Archaeology and this remains the definitive work on these eleventh-century objects. Stirrup-strap mounts functioned as a link between the metal stirrup and the stirrup strap, as David's drawing of the Chalgrove (Oxfordshire) stirrup illustrates. They tend to be triangular or rectangular in plan (although diamond and cross-shaped also occur) with rounded loop at the apex and a flange at the base of the reverse through which the leather strap was secured against an iron fitting. David identified several distinct types based on their form and decoration, which can be anthropomorphic, zoomorphic, scrolled/interlace or openwork. This example from Old Windsor depicts a lion, front paw raised and head thrown back in a roar (Williams' Class A, type 11A).

Above left: Stirrup-strap mount from Old Windsor. 46.8 mm high.

Above right: Chalgrove stirrup showing how the mounts would have functioned. (Illustration by David Williams, reproduced by kind permission of the Council for British Archaeology and Marged Haycock)

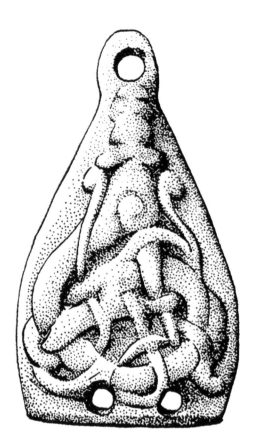

BERK-3EB585 from Hampstead Norreys next to an illustration of a similar mount showing the decoration. (Illustration by David Williams, reproduced by kind permission of the Council for British Archaeology and Marged Haycock)

Examples of other stirrup-strap mounts, left to right: BERK-30DB18 from Englefield, BERK-6F9608 from Speen, BERK-20B4E4 from Shaw, and SUR-419AD2 from Cookham.

Chapter 6
The Medieval Period
(AD 1066 – 1500)

After the Norman Conquest of AD 1066, William the Conqueror constructed a motte-and-bailey castle 3 km away from the royal residence of Old Windsor, where Edward the Confessor had held court until he died earlier that year. Over the centuries Windsor Castle was rebuilt, initially in stone in the twelfth century, and it continued to expand and grow. By the sixteenth century stone from the dissolved Reading Abbey and Wallingford Castle was used in construction. Windsor Castle, in its various guises, has been a royal residence on and off for nearly 1,000 years. Wallingford Castle (then in Berkshire) was built in the mid-eleventh century and had its own mint until *c.* AD 1250. After the castle fell into disuse it was finally destroyed by Oliver Cromwell in the seventeenth century.

In 1215 King John and the barons signed the Magna Carter at Runnymede, a few miles from Windsor. Towns like Reading, which had modest populations at the time of the Conquest, started to grow and new settlements like Newbury were founded. Towns close to the Thames grew rapidly during the twelfth century, mostly due to the trade links the river offered. Ecclesiastical properties continued to grow in size and power, with some fourteen religious estates known of in the county. One of the most powerful was Abingdon Abbey (then in Berkshire), which became one of the wealthiest in the country. The Dissolution of the Monasteries by Henry VIII in AD 1538 resulted in the partial or near-complete destruction of religious houses such as Bisham, Reading and Abingdon. The last Abbot of Reading, Hugh Cook of Faringdon, was found guilty of high treason and executed in front of the abbey church.

The remains of Reading Abbey. (Image © Rod Trevaskus, reproduced with kind permission)

Religious items, or items depicting religious scenes, are not uncommon from the medieval period. Of octafoil form, the sides of this mount slope downwards from the face. The lamb faces right and the rounded head looks downwards; only two legs are visible. The tail extends halfway down the hind leg and the front leg joint is depicted as a short spiral. Behind the lamb is a staff surmounted by a cross with expanding terminals. Most of the gilding survives. The entire field is covered with closely spaced punched annulets which extend as far as a bordering groove. Four opposing lobes are pierced with a circular hole, one of which contains remains of a rivet. The reverse of the mount is not gilded.

The mount is of uncertain purpose but it may have decorated a casket. The mount depicts the Agnus Dei, the Lamb of God, a visual representation of Jesus as a lamb, and is often associated with St John the Baptist, who said of Jesus: 'Behold the Lamb of God that taketh away the sin of the world' (Gospel of St John 1:29). The Agnus Dei is usually depicted as a lamb carrying a flag rather than just a cross as in this example. The flag or pennant may have been an addition by crusading knights (the Knights Templar and Knights of St John), as it is often depicted as the flag of St George, a symbol still seen in pub signs. As for the date of this mount, the intensive use of punched annulets is often found on harness pendants from the twelfth century. The treatment of the leg joint is reminiscent of late Viking art, so taken together a date in the first half of the twelfth century, probably closer to *c.* AD 1100, would seem appropriate.

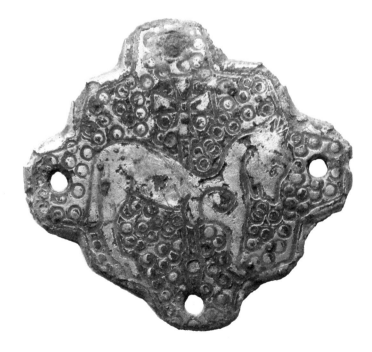

Gilded mount from
Shottesbrooke.
38 mm wide.

Example of the Agnus Dei on a medieval seal matrix from Porthcawl (NMGW-E91B83). The inscription reads: + S' FRATRIS BALDVINI: Seal of Brother Baldwin.

Lamb and Flag public house sign. (Image © Derek Harper, CC-BY-SA/2.0)

A seal matrix is used to make an impression on wax, acting much as a signature does on official documentation such as charters and land deeds. Of the 5,000 medieval matrices the PAS has recorded, most are impersonal 'off-the-shelf' matrices, featuring popular scenes from the period including religious depictions of, for example, St John the Baptist or the Virgin and Child. Others are humorous or cheeky – matrices depicting a squirrel with the legend '*I crake notis*' ('I crack nuts') may refer to sexual conquest. Others matrices name the owner, often in abbreviated form, and occasionally their place of origin. Silver and gold seal matrices are occasionally discovered but most are of copper alloy, like this example from Welford. Surviving in very good condition, the matrix is circular and has an integrally cast suspension loop on the reverse. The inscription on the front, around the outer circumference of the matrix, is easily read once imprinted. The inscription begins with a cross pattée and reads 'SIGILL.ROGERI.DE.MVLINS' (Seal of Roger De Mulins). There are two circular fields within this inscription, the first comprises a ring of dots and the second, the innermost field, contains a variation of a cross moline, or a cross ancrée – both Christian symbols.

Although we are not 100 per cent certain, this could well be the personal seal of Roger de Moulins, Grand Master of the Order of the Knights Hospitallers (later the Knights of St John), his 'secretum', his own seal, which could be used as a counterseal alongside the official seal of the Master of the Hospital. 'We know that Roger de Moulins was in England between February and mid-April AD 1184/85. He was present at a meeting of Henry II's court at Reading in February 1185, together with the Patriarch of Jerusalem, who consecrated the Temple Church in London on 10 February, and the Hospitallers' church at Clerkenwell on 10 March. So Roger de Moulins was at least in Berkshire in AD 1184/85. The main Hospitaller estate in Berkshire was at Greenham (in the old parish of Thatcham), the manor being granted by Maud, Countess of Clare, during the reign of Henry II' (Pamela Willis).

Although the seal was found to the west of Newbury it is possible that the seal was lost during de Moulin's visit to England. The seal is of a type that dates to the later twelfth century, which fits in nicely with de Moulin's visit to Berkshire in early AD 1184/85. De Moulin returned to Jerusalem but died from a lance wound inflicted during a battle against Saladin near Nazareth in May 1187. Later that year the Christians lost Jerusalem to the Saracen forces.

The seal of Roger de Moulins and its impression from Welford. 32 mm diameter.

Medieval wall painting of Roger de Moulin.
(Unknown artist; Wikimedia Commons)

Knights
Hospitaller
document seal
from Essex
(BH-8F07F3),
produced
under Amaury
d'Amboise, Master
of the order AD
1503–12.

Although debatable as to whether this find is 'portable' or not, the PAS records archaeological objects found by members of the public so this stone stoup qualified! Made of an unidentified stone and weighing close to 25 kg, the stoup was found among discarded building and stone rubble on a trackway in Ufton Nervet some forty years ago and has been in use as a bird bath ever since. A stoup is a bowl for holy water that would have stood by the entrance to a church. The faithful would dip their fingers into the water and make the sign of the cross as a reminder of their baptism, to cleanse venial sins and to protect against evil. This example is 160 mm high with the circular well in the centre *c.* 270 mm in diameter. Broadly oval in plan, the stoup has two carved vertical linear projections on opposing ends and chevron-shaped decoration on the sides, all in high relief. Although near-impossible to date with certainty, this stoup probably dates from *c.* AD 1100 – 1300. The finder conducted his own research into the stoup and discovered that several churches and chapels in the area have been demolished and/or rebuilt over the centuries, so unfortunately we'll never know from whence it came. However, it serves as a reminder that the life of some objects persist, even if their current use is somewhat different to the original intention.

Stone stoup from Ufton Nervet. The inner well is 270 mm diameter. (Courtesy of Richard J. Smith)

During the twelfth and thirteenth centuries a large and successful enamelling industry based at Limoges in France exported some very fine and distinctive objects across the Continent and to Britain. Metal objects were decorated using the champlevé technique (filling cells with vitreous enamel then firing the object), the subject often religious in nature. A good number of Limoges mounts have been recorded by the PAS, including panels from ecclesiastical crosses and reliquary mounts depicting saints and figurines of Christ. This worn medieval strap fitting was probably a buckle plate and is likely to have been made in Limoges. It is decorated in very low relief which was probably infilled with enamel, now missing. The design is quite worn and some areas are indistinct but depicts a man wearing a tunic, holding in one hand a sword and in the other a diamond-shaped shield, who stands astride an animal which doesn't appear to be horse. The form of the animal's head is unclear and only three legs are visible. The head of the man has been obscured by and replaced with a round-headed rivet. Traces of engraved bordering lines are just visible in places on the animal. In each of the two right-hand corners is a rivet hole, one of which is filled with a round-headed rivet. This is probably the upper part of a buckle plate. An item from Swaffham in Norfolk which retains much of the enamelling depicts a similar scene of a centaur, with the body of a lion rather than a horse.

Limoges buckle plate from Old Windsor with design interpretation. 38.2 mm high.

Comparable mount from Swaffham, Norfolk, retaining much of its enamel (NMS-B8B005).

A wing from a medieval reliquary, probably an angel's wing, found at Stanford Dingley (BERK-1E67A6). 90.3 mm long.

In AD 1121 William the Conqueror's youngest son, Henry I, founded Reading Abbey. It became one of the biggest and wealthiest monasteries in England and from 1125 the king granted the abbey the right to a mint and moneyer. This right appears to have been withdrawn during the reign of Henry III (AD 1216–72) and it wasn't until 1338, in the reign of Edward III, that Reading Abbey regained its minting rights. The abbey struck silver farthings, halfpennies and pennies. The fractions are incredibly rare – one halfpenny and only fifteen pennies of Edward III's Reading mint have been recorded on the PAS database; the coin from Cookham is the only PAS example found in Berkshire.

The Cookham coin has been bent in half in antiquity, probably purposefully (to either break it in half to create two 'unofficial' halfpennies, or possibly to act as a type of token). The coin has been re-straightened by the finder, a dangerous practice without specialist knowledge as all too often the coin will snap! Pennies of this period are often much worn and frequently clipped (a practice whereby a small section of the edge of the coin was removed to steal the silver). The one defining attribute of the Reading coins is the scallop shell in one quarter of the reverse, which is just visible in the Cookham example; the lettering on the reverse of the coin also gives the mint town (VILLA RADINGY). The Reading pennies were issued by John Stoke de Appleford, Abbot of Reading during Edward III's third 'florin' coinage of AD 1344–51. A unique Reading coin of the second coinage (probably struck in 1338) was purchased from a detectorist by a coin dealer in 1999 and later acquired by the Fitzwilliam Museum in Cambridge.

Reading mint penny of Edward III from Cookham (SUR-0EA84B). 18.8 mm diameter.

Reading mint penny from Cockermouth, Cumbria, showing scallop shell detail in the first quarter of the reverse (LANCUM-4F7D6F).

Wallingford (formerly in Berkshire) had its own mint and was striking coins from the reign of Æthelstan (from *c.* AD 927) until *c.* AD 1250, during the reign of Henry III when this coin, found at Thatcham, was struck (SUR-E9A7F7). The inscriptions read HENRICVS REX III / ROB/ ERT/ONW/A[..].

Papal bullae were lead seals used as a means of official authentication on papal documents sent out from Rome. They are uncommon finds and when they are found they are often worn and usually broken. A rare discovery was this group of three overleaf from Wokingham, found close to one another and probably deposited together sometime in the early fifteenth century AD.

All papal bullae follow the same format: the obverse depicts the heads of St Peter and St Paul below the inscription SPA SPE (SPA = *Sanctus Paulus*, SPE = *Sanctus Petrus*). St Paul looks right and St Peter looks left towards a cross between them. A beaded border encloses the design. On the reverse is the name of the Pope issuing the edict, usually over three lines and including the abbreviation 'PP' for *Papa Pontifex*. Bullae have a hole for a cord through the middle of the vertical axis. The cord could be tied or sealed around the parchment document; often bullae are broken through this weak point.

The first seal (BERK–47DE41) is of Pope Martin IV (AD 1281–85). It has a diameter of 35.9 mm and weighs 43.5 grams. This bulla is in the best condition of the three. The reverse legend reads MAR/TINVS/PP IIII. The second bulla (BERK-47FAF2) is of Boniface IX (AD 1389–1404) and is quite well-preserved, although slightly bent. It measures 36.4 mm in diameter and weighs 40.3 grams. The lettering BONI/FATIUS/PP VIIII is clear. The obverse has a tear in the lead around the upper cord hole, possibly caused by forcibly removing the cord. The third bulla (BERK–480137) is the most worn of the three. Issued by Pope Gregory IX (AD 1227–41), the lettering GRE/GORIVS/PP VIIII is clear enough, but slightly obscured by wear and corrosion. This bullae has a diameter of 38.8 mm and weighs 51.2 grams.

Tim Pestell (Curator, Norwich Castle Museum and Art Gallery) comments that: 'The discovery of three bullae so close together is a usual occurrence and suggests a deliberate deposition rather than a chance occurrence.' Other groups of bullae have been discovered but they represent a pope and their immediate successor. In these instances Pestell suggests that such caches '[are] suggestive of material that had ... been thrown away as a group, perhaps from clearing out a bundle of papal documents, at much the same time; they might even represent a group of documents hidden together and subsequently not recovered'. The Wokingham bullae span 123 years and why they should have been deposited together is unknown. More research of the findspot may reveal the answer.

Papal bullae from Wokingham: BERK-47DE41, BERK-47FAF2 and BERK–480137.

This beautiful fifteenth-century gold brooch was found while digging for worms to use for fishing. The brooch, which retains its fine gold rod pin, is circular in plan and decorated on the front with grooved cells alternately occupied by spheres and words from an inscription. The inscription is in French 'black letter' text and reads '*avez tout mon coer a vre plaisir*' ('have all my heart at your pleasure'). The reverse of the brooch is decorated with four-petalled flowers and sprigs of foliage. These elements would have originally been enamelled and the lettering may have been too but none now survives. The French inscription is common on jewellery of this date, as the language was still commonly used by the English aristocracy in letters and inscriptions; brooches with inscriptions are high-status objects and a good number of gold examples have been recorded with the PAS.

The finder took the brooch to his local FLO for identification thirty-five years after he first discovered it. As the object was over 300 years old and made of gold it was reported as Treasure, but it fell under the old law of Treasure Trove as it was discovered before the instigation of the replacement Treasure Act 1996. The ancient law of Treasure Trove stated that objects of gold or silver hidden with the intention of recovery and whose heirs are unknown would become property of the Crown. In this instance it is impossible to trace any heirs nor prove that the brooch was intended to be recovered, therefore it was classed as a casual loss and returned to the finder. Treasure Trove now mostly applies to objects under 300 years old.

Gold annular brooch from Swallowfield. External diameter is 32 mm.

Find 44. Iron stirrup from Cookham (SUR-2C2345)
AD 1450 – 1550

Stirrups had been in use in China since the Jin Dynasty (AD 264 – 420) but the technology didn't arrive in Western Europe until the early Middle Ages. The use of stirrups was an important development and their use changed mounted warfare, and may have even stimulated the evolution of the class of warrior knight. This complete iron stirrup of late medieval date from Cookham is a rare discovery, and not just because metal detectorists tend to discriminate against iron signals. Surprisingly well preserved and recovered around 1 foot below the surface, the stirrup is broadly pear shaped with slightly incurving sides. The sides are broad (40 mm at their base) and are decorated with fan-like ribbing which extends around halfway up the side. The raised footrest and the ribbing on the sides are both familiar on the broad D-shaped stirrups of the early sixteenth century. One side appears to be slightly distorted but this may be intentional and would suggest it has been made for a right foot. At its apex the stirrup expands slightly to accommodate a slot of 28 mm for the stirrup leather.

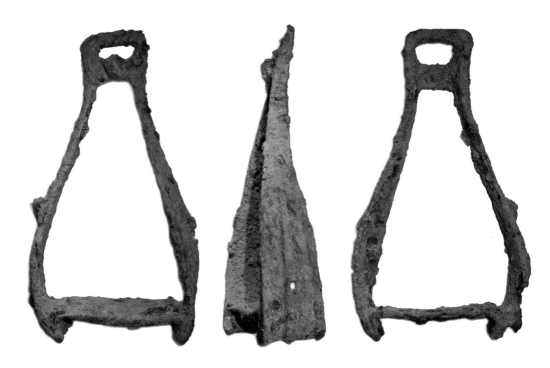

Iron stirrup from Cookham. 200.2 mm high.

Chapter 7
The Post-Medieval Period (AD 1500 – 1900)

Find 45. Purse bar from Inkpen (BERK-31F9D9)
AD 1450 – 1550

Purses and pouches were worn during the late medieval period to carry coins, religious trinkets and other small personal items. They were worn by both men and women and were often tied around the waist or hung from a belt at the waist either on view or concealed below skirts or under men's jackets. By the post-medieval period women wore 'pockets' beneath their skirts. For women, the slits in petticoats enabled easy access to the pockets and their contents. The term 'pickpocket' thus comes from street thieves cutting the laces securing a lady's pocket or man's wallet. Purses were generally worn on display, complementing an individual's clothing and indicating status or wealth. They usually consisted of a metal crossbar with loop for suspension and a metal hoop to which the fine leather or textile bag could be sewn.

This copper alloy purse bar from Inkpen dates from *c.* AD 1450 – 1550. The bar is short compared to other examples and has a large central rectangular boss, ribbed arms and terminals with rounded knops. Only a fragment of the hoop of the hanging frame is retained, seen around one arm of the purse bar. The long pendant loop is fixed through the purse bar boss and still swivels freely; it has a large rounded knop at the base and a flat-sectioned neck that fits through the hole in the boss. Three raised collars separate the neck from the loop itself. The boss is decorated on either face with deeply incised diagonal scores; on other examples this type of decoration is filled with a black metallic inlay called niello (see SUR-0E4225).

David Williams had been studying and researching late medieval purses for several years before his death. His work offered clarification, dating and a new classification of purses over that published by Ward-Perkins in 1940. His work was published posthumously in 2018, becoming the fiftieth Datasheet issued by the Finds Research Group. The Inkpen purse is a Williams Class C1.

Purse bar from Inkpen. 59.6 mm high, 53 mm wide.

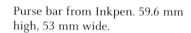

Another style of purse bar, missing its suspension loop, found at Arborfield (SUR-0E4225). 155 mm long.

A near-complete purse from Cobham in Surrey with a frame diameter of 128 mm (SUR-7C8248).

Gold coins of any period are not common finds. This small hoard, or 'purse-drop', was found in woodland near Frilsham. The coins are in near-perfect condition, suggesting that they were found where they were dropped in the 1620s. Consisting of three gold coins of James I of England (James VI of Scotland), the coins are all over 90 per cent gold. The earliest coin is a Scottish sword and sceptre piece with a fineness of 22 carats weighing 5.02 grams. Issued in 1601, before James ascended the English throne after the death of Elizabeth I in 1603, it had a value of 120 shillings Scots when issued, equivalent to 10 shillings sterling. The remaining coins are English issues, a unite of the second issue (dating from 1612–13), weighing 9.91 grams, and a laurel of the third issue (dating from 1621–23), weighing 9.03 grams. The two English coins were each worth £1 sterling (20 shillings) when they were issued. Barrie J. Cook of the Department of Coins and Medals at the British Museum comments in his report that:

> Due to shifting gold prices ... the value of the Second Coinage unite had been enhanced to 22 shillings in 1612 and the laurel was introduced at a lower weight to provide a £1 coin again. The Scottish coin's value would have been similarly raised in England to 11 shillings. These coins would have been in currency together and, with a face-value of £2 13s in the years [they were dropped] represent a considerable sum of money at the time, equivalent to several months' income for an ordinary labourer or artisan.

These coins were declared Treasure by the Berkshire coroner and are being acquired by West Berkshire Museum.

The three Frilsham gold coins of James VI/I, dropped *c.* 1620s. Sword and Sceptre piece (26 mm diameter).

Frilsham gold coins. Top: Unite (35 mm diameter); below: Laurel (32 mm diameter).

One of David Williams' favourite artefacts of recent years was this humorously indecent toy dating from *c*. AD 1600 – 1800. David very much enjoyed writing this find up, and the description that follows is an edited version of his report:

The object depicts a bawdy representation of a copulating couple who stand facing each other. Each figure has a hand rested on the others' shoulder and the hands secured to the opposing figure by a rivet through each hand. Both partners are depicted in a somewhat naive and un-naturalistic fashion; the lower limbs of the male in particular are out of proportion to the torso, and the head is tiny in comparison to the remainder of the body. The female stands wearing a floor-length dress, which is divided and drawn back to expose the front lower body below the waist. Her legs are divided by a wide tapering groove at the apex of which is a round hole which represents the vagina and curving lines intended to represent pubic hair. The breasts are depicted as small, but prominent and pointed. Facial features comprise a single groove for the mouth and a pair of drilled pits for the eyes. She wears a head covering of a plain encircling band above which is a rounded form with three diagonal grooves, possibly hair but more likely a form of hat.

Bawdy toy from
Swallowfield.
100 mm high.

The male figure comprises two main elements; the upper body is attached to the lower part by means of a separate pin. The lower part of the body passes through a rectangular cut-out on the platform on which the female stands and is fixed in position by means of a separate rivet through his legs above the ankles. No attempt has been made to show separate legs. The male's booted feet with high heels project below the platform, giving the impression of this figure hanging in mid-air and this position results in the head of the male being positioned below the head of the female, although his body is in reality considerably longer. The male wears a short waist-length jacket. Little of the man's head can be seen below a wide-brimmed cylindrical hat. As with the female, eyes and mouth are shown by drilled pits and a groove. From a socket below the man's waist projects a separate rod which represents the erect penis. While the articulating waist and ankles are presently locked in position the figure of the male was clearly intended to rock back and forth to imitate sexual intercourse. This object falls within a range of other bawdy objects, mainly pipe tampers, which were no doubt used to titillate and amuse. Bawdy scenes were important features of eighteenth-century popular art, literature, and material culture.

Left: Pipe tamper from Stanford Dingley (BERK-1E0625). 66.2 mm high.

Right: Pipe tamper depicting a female urinating, from Dorney (SWYOR-C3DE5C). 58 mm high.

The first English Civil War (AD 1642–49) was a tumultuous and bloody conflict that affected the entire county. Politicians and the public alike were divided in their support for King Charles I (the Royalists, or 'Cavaliers') and Parliament (Parliamentarians, or 'Roundheads'). Berkshire saw three large and decisive battles fought within its bounds: the two Battles of Newbury (1643 and 1644) and the Seige of Reading (14–27 April 1643). Reading was under the control of a small garrison of Royalist troops (*c.* 2,000) and was besieged by 20,000 Parliamentarians who stationed themselves around the town and at Caversham Bridge to prevent Royalist reinforcements from Oxford reaching the garrison. Bombarded by cannon, the Reading garrison surrendered and retreated to Oxford. For two days afterwards the Parliamentarian troops ransacked the town. A possible remnant of the siege is this iron artillery ball found in a garden in Henry Street. Now in a corroded state, the ball weighs 0.9 lbs (406 grams) and is 1.96 inches (49.9 mm) in diameter. Such shot would be fired from a falconet, a piece of light field artillery with a calibre of 2 inches, firing shot of approximately 1 lb to a maximum distance of around 2,000 yards. The falconet cannon came into use during the latter half of the fifteenth century and was mounted on four wheels to make it more mobile on the field of battle. They were widely used during the Civil War.

Cannonball from Reading. 49.9 mm diameter.

Lead carbine shots from Shaw, probably related to the Second Battle of Newbury (BERK-1B5857). 22–23 grams each.

Civil War period iron trigger mechanism for a flintlock pistol from Newbury (BERK-4E24C3). 72.2 mm long.

Toy cannons were very popular from the late sixteenth to nineteenth centuries and were still advertised for sale in late Victorian trade catalogues. These miniature replicas were produced as complete working models of their larger counterparts and were capable of firing a small charge. This example from Winkfield is 100 mm in length, 31.59 mm across the trunnions and 16.68 mm across the cascabel. The trunnions sat in the top of the cheeks of a gun carriage and enabled the piece to be elevated. The touch hole can be seen forward of the cascobel. A muzzle-loading piece – a small charge of black powder – could be inserted into the gun then fired by lighting the powder through the touch hole. This was not without danger though – the lower side of the cannon has been impressively ripped apart between the trunnions and the raised band from the force of an accidental explosion. Although these are often described as toys, it is possible that these working miniature cannon may not have been toys for children but may have been used by adults. Dating for this example remains uncertain but in general terms the cannon appears to be of eighteenth-century style.

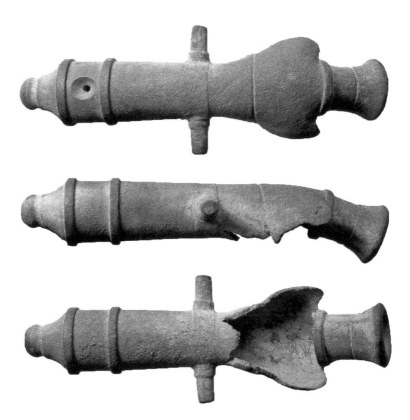

Toy cannon
from Winkfield.
100 mm long.

Eighteenth-century 'toy' cannon on a reconstruction naval carriage. (Image © Michael Byard)

Early seventeenth-century toy gun, capable of firing a small charge. From Swallowfield (SUR-CED9E7). 76 mm long.

Although the PAS tends not to record objects that post-date *c.* AD 1700 (and earlier for coins), there are some items of historical interest or local importance that do merit recording. One such class of object is militia buttons, something David Williams was keen on recording and encouraged others to do the same.

The militia were local groups of part-time soldiers formed after the instigation of the Militia Act of 1757. It was compulsory for county and parish officials to keep a list of eligible fighting men over eighteen years of age until AD 1831, after which any service was voluntary. During the eighteenth century, when Britain was often at war with France and Holland, the militias were intended to be the standing homeland defence force. This silver-plated copper alloy button bears the legend ROYAL HAMPSHIRE VOLUNTEERS around a crown. Comparative examples suggests a manufacture date of *c.* 1794–1802. Finding information on this regiment has proved difficult; there were a few infantry volunteer regiments fighting in the War of American Independence (1775–83), and 'Royal Lancasters Volunteers' is one that is listed, but there is no mention of the Hampshires. The Volunteer & Militia lists for 1794, 1796, 1797, 1799, 1800 and 1801 have all been checked and no unit of this title is listed. Also, the Parliamentary Return for 9 and 13 December 1803, which lists many units that didn't make it into the April 1804 War Office List, have been searched, but again no such unit is listed. It has been suggested that the Royal Hampshire Volunteers was an infantry of the line regiment, several of which are yet to be identified.

Royal Hampshire Volunteers militia button.
17.3 mm diameter.

Militia buttons: Oxfordshire 12th Regiment of Militia, found at Kintbury (BERK-15D74C), Sussex Volunteers, found at Wokingham Without (SUR-DF424E), Twickenham Volunteers found at Cox Green (SUR-8CEEB0).

Final Thoughts

David Wynn Williams had worked for the PAS since 2003. He was a loyal colleague, always ready to respond to a call for help from his fellow FLOs, whether it be attending a rally miles away from his own home or excavating an *in situ* find. David was passionate about forging good relationships with both finders and landowners. At rallies he was often to be seen walking the fields, chatting to finders and encouraging them to record their finds, of which David recorded around 16,500 in his time with the PAS. He had many loyal finders and David always had time for them, not just to record their finds but as good friends. David was an involved member and great supporter of the Finds Research Group and contributed a number of datasheets, most notably those on 'Stirrup Terminals' and 'Anglo-Scandinavian Horse Harness Fittings'. Probably his best-known publication among finds specialists is the regularly thumbed CBA Research Report 'Late Saxon Stirrup-Strap Mounts'. David was a talented illustrator and all his publications are self-illustrated. He was also a Fellow of the Society of Antiquaries. David leaves a large hole in PAS and we miss him very much. (Written by Katie Hinds, FLO for Hampshire, and Anni Byard).

David Wynn Williams: 31 August 1949 –
9 December 2017.

Further Reading

All of the finds featured in this book, and the other 10,000-odd finds recorded from Berkshire, are available to view freely on the PAS database: www.finds.org.uk/database. You can search by period, artefact type and region/parish. Findspot locations are automatically restricted to a four-figure grid reference (1 km square). The website also provides information on the Treasure Act 1996, suggested research projects, contact details and how to get involved.

Below are a handful of lay book recommendations which are a good starting point for the interested reader:

Coombs, T., Ridout Sharpe, J., Davies, H., Harrison, A., Byard, A., 'Land of the Atrebates; In and around Roman Berkshire' (*Berkshire Archaeological Journal* No. 83, Berkshire Archaeology Society, 2018).

Dils, J., Yates, M. (eds), *An Historical Atlas of Berkshire* (Second edition) (Berkshire Record Society, 2012).

Hutt, A., Goodenough, P., Pyne, V., *Living in the Iron Age in and around Berkshire* (*Berkshire Archaeological Journal* No. 78, Berkshire Archaeology Society, 2010).

Moorhead, S., *A History of Roman Coinage in Britain* (Greenlight Publishing, 2013).

Thames Valley Landscapes Monograph, *Thames Through Time: The Archaeology of the Gravel Terraces of the Upper and Middle Thames,* Vols 1–3 (Lancaster, 2007, 2009, 2011). Various authors.

Williams, D., *Late Saxon Stirrup-Strap Mounts: A Classification and Catalogue* (Council for British Archaeology Research Report 111, 1999).

Worden, B., *The English Civil Wars, 1640–1660* (Phoenix, 2010).